The Protection Bible

THE ESSENTIAL BOOK OF

Protection

SPELLS AND

Magic

Beatrice Aurelia Crowley

Erebus Society

Erebus Society

First published in Great Britain in 2025
Erebus Society

First Edition

ISBN: 978-1-912461-63-9

www.ErebusSociety.com

Table of Contens

What is Protection Magic?

INTRODUCTION

Within the expansive domain of witchcraft, protective magic serves as a fundamental element—a source of security and empowerment for its practitioners. It is the ancient practice of crafting shields, both visible and invisible, to protect against injury, misfortune, and malicious entities. Throughout history, witches have utilised this powerful branch of magic to protect themselves, their loved ones, their homes, and their sacred areas.

Protection magic transcends a simple assemblage of spells or rituals; it embodies a deep connection to the natural and spiritual forces that envelop us. This artwork invokes the fundamental forces of earth, air, fire, and water, intricately combining them with purpose and concentration to create an invulnerable shield against negativity. Whether casting a circle of light, inviting heavenly guardians, or creating a charm infused with protective energy, each act in protection magic represents a holy affirmation of your autonomy and security.

What renders protective magic vital to the practice? It is the certainty that, regardless of life's adversities or lingering shadows, you possess the ability to establish a sanctuary. By learning this discipline of magic, you acquire the power to safeguard against exterior dangers while cultivating the inner fortitude that wards off fear and susceptibility.

Protective magic is both multifaceted and essential. It can protect against bad energy, neutralise mental attacks, and repel evil intents directed against you. This craft provides a diverse array of techniques, ranging from ancient amulets and magical sigils to intricate rituals that invoke the elements, all aimed at ensuring your safety. Its core resides in the witch's intent—a concentrated will that converts ordinary tools into vessels of significant power.

What is protective magic, and what is its mechanism of action? To comprehend it fully, we must explore its origins, its traditions, and the enigmatic forces it wields. Let us commence this investigation, where ancient wisdom converges with the witch's steadfast will, to unveil the secrets of this vital trade.

UNDERSTANDING PROTECTION MAGIC

Protection magic is an enduring discipline that intertwines intention, energy, and mysticism to construct potent barriers against harm. At its core is the capacity to direct your will and concentration into defensive energies that shield against many threats—whether physical, emotional, or spiritual. This method involves the manipulation of energies, utilising elements, the natural environment, and invisible worlds to create barriers that protect individuals, residences, and sacred locations from negativity and harmful influences.

Protection magic, whether as a luminous energy sphere around you, a safeguard inscribed at your home's entrance, or a mystical amulet near your heart, is the pinnacle of self-empowerment. For ages, witches have utilised this skill to protect themselves and their loved ones, assuring safety amidst a world rife with hidden dangers and energetic disturbances.

The core of protective magic resides in its adaptability. It may range from a whispered incantation said in a time of necessity to a complex ritual incorporating symbols, candles, and sacred implements. Every action, regardless of its magnitude or nuance, is infused with the purpose of deterring undesirable influences. Negative energies, psychic assaults, curses, and spiritual disruptions are only shadows that diminish in the presence of a robust protection spell.

Engaging in protective magic entails assuming the role of a guardian for your personal sanctuary. The formation of a shield—conceived as a luminous dome, an invulnerable wall of flames, or an intricate array of sacred symbols—is a profoundly personal and transforming endeavour. This barrier not only deflects danger but also enhances the witch's abilities, acting as a perpetual reminder of their intrinsic power and link to global energies.

The techniques of protective magic are as diverse as the witches who employ them. Some invoke the stabilising force of the soil for protection, while others utilise the purifying properties of water to eliminate negativity. Fire kindles the flames of bravery and defence, while air disperses detrimental forces through its rapid currents. In addition to the elements, crystals, herbs, and symbols frequently function as conduits, enhancing the witch's intention and grounding the protective energies.

Protection magic transcends mere defence; it signifies a proclamation of dominion over one's area and spirit. Engaging in its practice signifies assuming the role of custodian of your own fate, manipulating the surrounding energies to foster harmony and security. This craft is a source of power for those who wield it with clarity and purpose, whether to shield against daily interruptions or to protect against deeper threats.

THE ESSENCE OF PROTECTION MAGIC

Protection magic fundamentally embodies a sacred guardianship—a proclamation of dominion over the surrounding forces. This practice is founded on an enduring aspiration for safety, peace, and well-being. Protection magic harnesses the essential energies of existence, crafting formidable shields that defend the practitioner or designated target from injury. These shields, created with purpose and infused with terrestrial and celestial energy, serve as a lasting witness to the witch's determination and expertise in the art.

Protection magic is intricately linked to the natural world, deriving power from the earth's stability, the winds' watchfulness, the purifying waters, and the transformational fire. The elements function as allies, each providing distinct attributes that strengthen the protective barrier. This magic transcends the earthly realm, drawing upon the illuminating presence of celestial bodies—the sun's brilliance, the moon's vigilant luminescence, and the constellations' timeless knowledge—to enhance its potency.

This type of magic represents a nuanced equilibrium between proactivity and reaction. It enables witches to perceive the faint indications of impending peril before they escalate, facilitating proactive measures. Protection magic serves as a sentry, consistently guarding against negativity and harm through the creation of wards, talismans, or sigils. It concurrently enables the practitioner to react promptly to imminent threats, counteract curses, eliminate psychic assaults, and neutralise malicious intentions.

The fundamental nature of safeguarding Magic transcends mere defence; it constitutes an act of empowerment. By controlling these forces, witches not only repel danger but also exert control over their surroundings and establish their entitlement to tranquilly and refuge. This practice cultivates resilience, both against external challenges and within the practitioner's heart and spirit. It cultivates confidence and security, serving as a reminder that safety resides within the witch's grasp and the energies they wield.

Protection magic is a fluid power, according to the demands of the situation. A murmured incantation can protect a voyage, whilst an intricate ceremony can save an entire domicile. A solitary rune inscribed on paper can serve as a silent guardian, while a deliberately designed circle can sanctify a location, protecting it from all evil. Every act of protective magic exemplifies the witch's ingenuity and purpose, establishing a connection between the tangible and the ethereal realms.

Protection magic serves as a symbol of hope and a defence against disorder. It provides the certainty that, amid global challenges, we have the ability to create environments of safety and tranquilly. Through this sacred art, the witch serves as both a protector and a mentor, ensuring that the forces of light triumph against darkness. Allow its power to permeate your being, and may its energy steadfastly protect your journey.

KEY ELEMENTS OF PROTECTION MAGIC

1. Intent and Focus: The cornerstone of any defensive incantation is the witch's intent. A lucid and concentrated mind is essential to guarantee the spell is aimed precisely and efficiently. The objective must be to safeguard and defend against danger, without inflicting pain on others.

2. Instruments and Emblems: Frequently utilised instruments in protective magic encompass candles, crystals, herbs, and protecting emblems such as pentagrams, circles, and runes. These things are selected for their intrinsic defensive attributes and their capacity to enhance the witch's energies.

3. Chants and Incantations: Articulating the protection spell using chants and incantations aids in concentrating energy and reinforcing intent. These words frequently rhyme to establish a rhythmic cadence, augmenting the spell's potency.

4. Visualisation: Visualising the protective barrier is an essential element. The witch must observe the formation of a robust and impenetrable shield surrounding the target, repelling any bad effects.

COMMON USES OF PROTECTION MAGIC

1. Personal Protection: Establishing a barrier to repel bad energy, psychological assaults, and physical threats. This can be achieved by regular rituals, the use of protective amulets, or the visualisation of a protective bubble.

2. Home Protection: Employing spells and charms to defend one's residence against intruders, malevolent spirits, and detrimental energies. This may involve affixing protective symbols to doors and windows, use purifying herbs such as sage, or establishing wards around the premises.

3. Safeguarding Others: Enacting protection incantations for cherished individuals, guaranteeing their safety and welfare. This frequently entails the fabrication of charms or amulets that the individual can possess or adorn.

4. Spiritual Protection: Safeguarding against spiritual and psychic dangers, including curses, hexes, and evil entities. This may entail utilising protecting minerals, forming a salt circle, or invoking protective deities.

ORIGINS AND LORE

Ancient Egypt:

In the illuminated realms of ancient Egypt, protective magic was intricately integrated into everyday existence. Amulets embellished with sacred symbols, such the Eye of Horus and the Ankh, were valued not merely as ornaments but as formidable protections against malicious entities. The Egyptians thought these symbols transmitted heavenly energy, bestowing gifts of health, vitality, and safety.

Protective spells were inscribed on papyrus scrolls, engraved in stone, or carved into tomb walls to guarantee safe transit into the afterlife. Deities like as Bastet, the formidable lioness who defended against disorder, and Sekhmet, the ardent goddess of warfare and healing, were summoned through rituals and offerings to safeguard residences, families, and holy sites. The Egyptians amalgamated craftsmanship, faith, and magic in their pursuit of protection, bequeathing a legacy that endures as a source of inspiration.

Greek and Roman Traditions:

The ancient Greeks and Romans adopted protective magic, frequently integrating it with their worship of the deities. Sacred symbols such as the Greek Key (Meander), signifying infinity and oneness, were inscribed on jewellery and domestic objects to protect against malevolent spirits. The Roman Fascinum, a phallic amulet, was utilised as a powerful talisman to repel the "evil eye," a conviction in harmful stares that could induce misfortune.

Invocations to protective deities were prevalent, with gods like Athena, the embodiment of wisdom, and Mars, the protector of soldiers, were summoned for safeguarding in combat and everyday existence. Ordinary objects, such as a fragment of iron or a protective amulet, were transformed into potent instruments when infused with purpose and divine favour, embodying the conviction that the commonplace might be elevated to the extraordinary.

Celtic Traditions:

The Celts derived their guardianship from the natural world, using the energy of sacred trees, stones, and symbols to formulate powerful protective magic. The oak, a symbol of strength and resilience, and the rowan, referred to as the "witch's tree," were esteemed for their capacity to ward against malevolence. Branches from these trees were fashioned into wands or interlaced into charms, providing a concrete link to the elemental energies of the ground.

Complex knots and spirals, commonly found in Celtic art, functioned as protective symbols, with their continuous patterns thought to ensnare and disorient malevolent energy. The Celts' profound respect for the elements influenced their magic, with rituals frequently conducted at hallowed wells, hilltops, and woods to invoke the land's spirits for protection.

Mediaeval and Renaissance Europe:

Throughout the mediaeval and Renaissance periods, protective magic developed by integrating mystical traditions with religious beliefs and nascent sciences such as alchemy. Witches and cunning folk served as protectors of their communities, creating charms and amulets, formulating herbal medicines, and forming protective circles to repel malevolence.

Salt, representing purity and preservation, was scattered at doorways to deter malicious spirits, while holy water and imprinted charms with sacred texts were employed to protect homes and persons. The amalgamation of Christian symbols with ancient magical techniques resulted in distinctive protective forms, shown by the incorporation of pentacles with crosses, fostering a syncretic methodology that integrated both traditional and contemporary elements.

African and Diasporic Traditions:

Protection magic occupies a revered position in African traditional religions and its diasporic equivalents, like Hoodoo and Vodou. These traditions utilise personal artefacts, medicines, and religious symbols to build protection charms and spells. In Vodou, veves—elaborate, sacred symbols—are inscribed to summon the protection of lwa (spirits), establishing spiritual defences against harm.

Hoodoo techniques frequently entail the creation of protective mojo bags, containing plants such as angelica root or black salt, together with personal artefacts like hair or nail clippings, to shield against curses and hexes. These traditions represent a profound link to ancestors and the spiritual realm, merging practicality with deep devotion.

Contemporary Methods:

In the modern era, protective magic persists, its ancient origins evolving to meet current need. Contemporary witches utilise old techniques alongside innovative instruments, like digital sigils and defensive grids crafted from crystals such as black tourmaline, obsidian, and selenite.

The practice of casting circles continues to be fundamental in protection rituals, however these hallowed spaces may now include incense, candle magic, and contemporary music to establish the ambiance. The old practice of creating amulets has transformed into the development of protective applications aimed at safeguarding against online negativity, illustrating the evolution of protection magic while maintaining its fundamental objective.

Mythology and Folklore:

The mythology of protection magic is rich, featuring enchanted artefacts and supernatural guardians that frequently assume crucial roles. Perseus, equipped with a mirrored shield bestowed by Athena, utilised Medusa's lethal gaze against her, exemplifying protection via cleverness and divine favour.

In Norse mythology, Thor's hammer, Mjölnir, served as both a weapon and a symbol of protection, sanctification, and might. These narratives evoke the persistent conviction in the protective and safeguarding capabilities of magic, resonating across time as a wellspring of inspiration and hope.

Magical Correspondences

HERBS

Herbs have historically been esteemed for their natural powers, encapsulating the essence of the soil and acting as potent partners in protective magic. Each herb possesses distinct vibrations that can be utilised to protect against harm, eliminate negativity, and strengthen personal and sacred spaces. The following is a brief compilation of herbs and their associations for protection:

ANGELICA ROOT

Element: Fire

Planet: Sun

Uses: A potent protective herb, particularly against hexes and curses. Often carried as a charm or burned to cleanse spaces.

BASIL

Element: Fire

Planet: Mars

Uses: Wards off evil spirits, protects against curses, and brings prosperity alongside safety. Often placed near windows or doorways to prevent harmful energies from entering.

BAY LEAVES

Element: Fire

Planet: Sun

Uses: Offers protection and strength. Writing intentions on bay leaves and burning them releases powerful protective energy.

BLACKBERRY LEAVES

Element: Earth

Planet: Venus

Uses: Used in protective spells for the home and to guard against spiritual attacks.

CHAMOMILE

Element: Water

Planet: Sun

Uses: Guards against evil spirits and enhances the energy of other protective herbs in spells and rituals.

CINNAMON

Element: Fire

Planet: Sun

Uses: Adds energy to protection spells, wards off negativity, and promotes safety in travel.

GARLIC

Element: Fire

Planet: Mars

Uses: A powerful ward against evil spirits and curses. Garlic is often hung in doorways to protect households.

HOLLY

Element: Fire

Planet: Mars

Uses: A sacred herb for warding off evil spirits and providing protection to the home, particularly during winter.

HYSSOP

Element: Fire

Planet: Jupiter

Uses: Purifies and protects against malevolent forces. Often burned or added to cleansing baths.

LAVENDER

Element: Air

Planet: Mercury

Uses: Calms the spirit while repelling negativity. Protects homes and promotes harmony within protective spaces.

MANDRAKE ROOT

Element: Earth

Planet: Mercury

Uses: Highly potent for protection, especially against dark spirits and harmful magic. Often carried or buried near doorways.

MUGWORT

Element: Earth

Planet: Venus

Uses: Guards against nightmares and psychic attacks, enhances intuition, and shields during divination.

PEPPERMINT

Element: Air

Planet: Mercury

Uses: Clears the mind, protects the spirit, and repels negativity. Peppermint is also used for travel protection.

ROSEMARY

Element: Fire

Planet: Sun

Uses: Guards against nightmares, promotes restful sleep, and strengthens the mind. Often hung over doorways or burned as incense for protection.

RUE

Element: Fire

Planet: Mars

Uses: Known as the "herb of grace," it is highly effective for protection against the evil eye and curses.

SAGE

Element: Air

Planet: Jupiter

Uses: Cleanses spaces of negativity, purifies the aura, and protects against psychic attacks. Burning sage is a traditional method of clearing and warding.

STINGING NETTLE

Element: Fire

Planet: Mars

Uses: Deflects curses and hexes, wards off unwanted energies, and strengthens personal power.

THYME

Element: Air

Planet: Venus

Uses: Protects against grief and sorrow, cleanses spaces of residual negativity, and strengthens the home's energy.

WORMWOOD

Element: Fire

Planet: Mars

Uses: Protects against psychic attacks and harmful spirits. Often burned to cleanse and shield spaces.

YARROW

Element: Water

Planet: Venus

Uses: Protects against negative influences, strengthens boundaries, and enhances courage. Often carried in sachets or placed at entryways.

CRYSTALS AND MINERALS

Crystals and minerals are primordial protectors, originating from the earth's core and infused with potent vibrations. They function as channels of energy, enhancing intention and providing protection against harm. The following is a brief compilation of their names, properties, and their associations for protection:

AMETHYST

Element: Air

Chakra: Third Eye, Crown

Uses: Shields against spiritual threats, enhances intuition, and promotes a sense of calm while protecting the aura.

BLACK TOURMALINE

Element: Earth

Chakra: Root

Uses: Absorbs and transmutes negative energy, protects against psychic attacks, and creates an energetic shield around the wearer.

BLUE KYANITE

Element: Water

Chakra: Throat

Uses: Shields against unwanted communication and psychic interference, creating a peaceful energy field.

CARNELIAN

Element: Fire

Chakra: Sacral

Uses: Shields against envy and anger, promotes courage, and invigorates protective energies.

CARNELIAN AGATE

Element: Fire

Chakra: Sacral

Uses: Guards against envy and jealousy, providing courage and vitality in protection spells.

CHRYSOPRASE

Element: Water

Chakra: Heart

Uses: Protects against emotional manipulation and promotes balance and harmony in protective workings.

CLEAR QUARTZ

Element: Air

Chakra: Crown

Uses: Amplifies protective energy and acts as a master healer, cleansing negativity from the surroundings and the self.

FLUORITE

Element: Air

Chakra: Third Eye

Uses: Shields against psychic manipulation and strengthens mental clarity, creating a fortress for the mind.

HEMATITE

Element: Earth

Chakra: Root

Uses: Grounds and stabilises energy, strengthens physical and emotional boundaries, and reflects negativity away.

JET

Element: Earth

Chakra: Root

Uses: A traditional stone for protection from curses and psychic attacks. Often worn as jewellery.

LABRADORITE

Element: Water

Chakra: Third Eye

Uses: Acts as a shield against psychic attacks and energy drain, while strengthening intuition and spiritual connection.

MALACHITE

Element: Earth

Chakra: Heart

Uses: Absorbs negative energies, protects against emotional harm, and shields the aura.

MOONSTONE

Element: Water

Chakra: Crown

Uses: Protects against psychic interference and provides emotional stability during tumultuous times.

OBSIDIAN

Element: Fire

Chakra: Root

Uses: A volcanic glass that repels negativity, dissolves blockages, and protects against emotional and psychic harm.

ONYX

Element: Earth

Chakra: Root

Uses: Absorbs and transforms negative energy while offering steadfast protection in times of uncertainty.

PYRITE

Element: Fire

Chakra: Solar Plexus

Uses: Protects against physical harm and creates a shield of confidence and strength.

RED JASPER

Element: Fire

Chakra: Root

Uses: Grounds energy while providing protection, particularly in chaotic or dangerous environments.

SELENITE

Element: Air

Chakra: Crown

Uses: Cleanses and protects spaces, enhances spiritual connection, and provides clarity while sealing energetic boundaries.

SMOKY QUARTZ

Element: Earth

Chakra: Root

Uses: Grounds the user, clears away negativity, and protects against unwanted influences.

TIGER'S EYE

Element: Fire

Chakra: Solar Plexus

Uses: Deflects negative energy and promotes courage, focus, and personal empowerment in the face of adversity.

Popular Charms Through History

Historically and culturally, numerous magical protection charms have been employed to shield persons from adverse energies and harmful entities. Presented below are several traditional charms and practices purported to provide protection:

MISTLETOE: THE AUREATE BRANCH

Mistletoe, commonly known as the golden bough, serves as a traditional Celtic protective amulet. Adherents of Celtic magic and practitioners of southern American folk magic transport mistletoe in a small, hand-stitched fabric pouch. This charm is thought to protect the bearer from danger and adverse effects.

MARJORAM: THE NEGATIVITY ABSORBER

Marjoram, sometimes referred to as wild oregano, is esteemed for its protective qualities. In Italian witchcraft, known as Stregheria, marjoram is ground into a powder and dispersed throughout the residence to absorb harmful negative energies. Furthermore, it is brewed as a tea and included into washing and cleaning water to safeguard the household and its occupants from harm.

SANTERIA: PURIFICATION CEREMONY

In Santeria, a folk religion observed in Cuba and Puerto Rico, adherents routinely incinerate brown sugar, a little amount of sulphur, and garlic powder on charcoal within their residences. This ceremony purges the residence of detrimental energy. After the dwelling is purified, a prayer to Santa Barbara, the patron saint of protection, is recited with the illumination of a red and a white candle to guarantee continued safeguarding.

POUCH WITH SULPHUR AND CAYENNE PEPPER

An uncomplicated yet potent charm entails carrying a little brown paper purse containing a pinch of sulphur powder and cayenne pepper, adorned with a drawn sword. This charm is said to repel hostile words and actions, offering protection against negativity. Bluing for Repelling Evil.

20

Plain bluing, historically employed to whiten laundry, is thought to ward off malevolent spirits in Southern American folklore. The bluing is contained in a little blue paper pouch to shield the wearer from bad entities.

CONSECRATED AMULET FOR SAFEGUARDING AND FORTUNE

To create a charm that provides protection and attracts luck, combine sulphur, blue metal stone (often utilised in concrete production), and bluing, then store the mixture in a blue fabric pouch. This combination is purported to concurrently repel malevolence and attract beneficial energies to the possessor.

MIRRORS AND BELLS: REPELLING MALEVOLENT SPIRITS

Mirrors are conventionally employed to ward off malevolent spirits. In Indian tradition, small fragments of silvered glass are stitched into cotton garments, accompanied by bells, to fulfil this function. The melodious chime of bells is very potent in repelling malevolent spirits. A small silver bell hung around the neck serves as a powerful protective talisman, particularly for travellers.

TRAVELER'S AMULET: REFLECTIVE SURFACE WITH ALLIUM

Travellers, frequently need additional protection, can gett advantage from a straightforward charm consisting of a small mirror coated with a clove of garlic. Positioning this mirror beneath the bed is said to safeguard the sleeper from danger when away from home. The mirror can be carried on one's person for continuous protection.

These protective charms, rooted in centuries of tradition and belief, provide a sense of security and well-being to their users. These charms, whether derived from the potency of plants, the resonance of bells, or the reflected qualities of mirrors, are valued instruments in the art of defensive magic.

Spells

Against Danger and Illness

REQUIREMENTS:

- ❀ **9** different fruits
- ❀ **9** votive candles
- ❀ **9** slices of eggplant
- ❀ **9** cents (coins)
- ❀ A piece of red cloth

INSTRUCTIONS:

Find a quiet, peaceful area where you won't be disturbed. Arrange the ingredients on a clean surface.

Place the **9** votive candles in a circle around you. Light them one by one, focusing on the intent of protection and cleansing.

Take each fruit and gently cleanse your body with it, starting from your head and moving down to your feet. As you do this, envision any danger and illness being absorbed by the fruit. Repeat with each of the **9** fruits.

Follow the same process with the **9** slices of eggplant.

Place the used fruits, eggplant slices, and **9** coins in the center of the red cloth. Wrap them securely, tying the cloth with a knot.

Hold the wrapped offerings in your hands and chant:

> *"Fruits of the earth, candles of light,*
> *Cleanse me of danger, banish my plight.*
> *Eggplant of healing, red cloth so bright,*
> *Protect me from illness, guard me through night."*

Travel to a long road near a cemetery. Find a discreet spot and gently place the wrapped offerings on the ground. As you leave, visualize the dangers and illnesses being carried away, replaced by a shield of protection and wellness.

Against Evil

This potent spell is intended to drive out negative energies and evil forces. You can make a protective talisman that can be worn to fend off danger by using a rusted nail and a hammer to invoke your intent.

REQUIREMENTS:

❁ A red, rusted nail (weathered by time and rain)
❁ A hammer
❁ A small shovel or trowel

PREPARATION:

This spell should be performed on the night of the new or no moon, a time for banishing and renewal.

INSTRUCTIONS:

Find a quiet and undisturbed place where you can perform this spell without interruptions. Arrange your tools on a small table or altar.

Hold the red, rusted nail in your hand. Feel its age and the power it has absorbed from the passing of time and rain.

With the hammer, strike the nail forcefully while shouting for the evil to depart. Channel all your energy and intent into the act. Chant:

"With each strike, I banish thee,
Evil forces, now you flee.
By this nail, both old and red,
Depart from here, your power shed."

Once you have hammered and chanted, take the nail outside. Bury it deeply in the ground under the night sky of the new moon. As you cover it with earth, chant:

"*In the earth, this nail shall lie,*
Banish evil, far and nigh.
Buried deep on moonless night,
Keep me safe, away from fright."

After some time has passed, return to the spot where you buried the nail. Dig it up with care.

Clean the nail if needed and wear it as a talisman of protection. Trust that it will shield you from evil forces.

NOTES

Ancient Greek Charmed Pendant

Through this ritual, the sun, water, and ancient deities' protection forces are infused into a charm or talisman. Make a potent charm of safety by charging the talisman in sunlight and calling forth divine protection.

REQUIREMENTS:

❁ A clear glass goblet
❁ Water
❁ A pinch of salt
❁ A charm or talisman (such as a gemstone pendant, a found stone, or any natural object)
❁ A chain or cord for the charm

INSTRUCTIONS:

Find a quiet and undisturbed place where you can perform this spell without interruptions. Arrange your ingredients and tools on a small table or altar in direct sunlight.

Fill the clear glass goblet halfway with water. Stir in a pinch of salt, mixing it thoroughly.

Place the goblet of saltwater in direct sunlight for approximately 15 minutes, allowing the water to absorb the sun's rays. Alongside the goblet, place the charm or talisman on a chain or cord to receive the sunlight as well.

After 15 minutes, take the goblet and talisman out of the sunlight. Dip the talisman into the water, letting it rest within the goblet. Using the chain or cord, gently swirl the talisman clockwise while chanting three times:

"Apollo's light, surround me bright,
Poseidon's waters, guard with might,
Athena's wisdom, guide my sight."

As you chant, imagine a beam of pure white light enveloping both the water and the talisman, infusing them with protective energy.

Leave the talisman in the water for another 10 minutes to fully absorb the protective energies.

After 10 minutes, remove the talisman from the water and gently dry it. Wear it with confidence, knowing it will protect you.

NOTES

Ancient Obsidian Protection

REQUIREMENTS:

❁ 1 white candle
❁ Tool for inscribing the candle
❁ Protection oil (or alternatives such as Lotus, Dragon's Blood, Frankincense, Sandalwood, or Rose Geranium)
❁ Lighter
❁ Candle holder
❁ 4 obsidian arrowheads (or obsidian, onyx, or apache tears stones)
❁ Any additional ritual items you feel necessary

INSTRUCTIONS:

Create your sacred circle, invoking your preferred protective deities or spirits.

Stand in the center of your circle, facing North. Hold the obsidian arrowheads (or stones) in your hand, and charge them with protective powers. Place them around the candle holder in each cardinal direction: North, East, South, and West.

Take the white candle and inscribe a pentagram onto it, along with your name or the name of the person you wish to protect.

Anoint the candle with your chosen protection oil, focusing intently on your need for protection. Visualize yourself being enveloped in a shield of divine safety. Feel and see yourself secure in all aspects of your life: home, car, workplace, and beyond.

Continue to charge the candle with your energy and intent until it feels vibrant and powerful, ready to burst with protective energy.

Place the candle in the holder and light it. Maintain your visualization or use your preferred techniques to send the protective energy outward.

When you feel the energy is fully sent, close your circle with gratitude to the deities or spirits you invoked. Allow the candle to burn down completely, solidifying the protection spell.

Chant:

> "By the power of obsidian's might,
> Protect me now, both day and night.
> With sacred flame and oil's embrace,
> Guard me well, in every place.
> Pentagram's shield, by name inscribed,
> Keep me safe. with power imbibed.
> Goddess and God, hear my plea,
> Wrap me in security.
> As this candle's light does wane,
> Protection's power shall remain."

The spell is now complete. Carry the feeling of protection with you, knowing you are safe and secure.

NOTES

Anti-Accident Spell

(FOR VEHICLES)

REQUIREMENTS:

❈ Strength Tarot card
❈ Small piece of copper wire
❈ Clover
❈ Star anise
❈ Catnip
❈ White cloth
❈ White candle
❈ Black ribbon
❈ Protection oil

PREPARATION:

Perform this spell on a Wednesday during the Waxing Moon while in the vehicle you wish to protect, parked in a quiet area.

INSTRUCTIONS:

Rub protection oil into the white candle, infusing it with your intent.

With the front door open, place the candle on the ground and light it.

Sit inside the car and imagine a triple white light of protection enveloping the vehicle. Visualize this light growing stronger and more radiant.

Sprinkle the clover, star anise, and catnip around the car, concentrating on the driver's side.

Take the copper wire and form it into the shape of a star. Place this star on the center of the vehicle's hood.

Visualize a safety net emanating from the copper star, encasing your vehicle. As you do so, chant the following:

Taliesin, Merlyn, Cerridwen,
Protect me now, your safeguard send.
Help me see clearly, on every street,
No accidents, no harm I meet.

Copper star, by fingers made,
Protect me now, by light displayed.
In your glow, I drive with might,
Guard me both by day and night.

East and South, West and North,
All directions, guard henceforth.

Place the herbs, copper star, tarot card, and any candle drips into the white cloth, gathering it into a small bag.

Tie the bag with the black ribbon and hang it inside the car, or place it under the driver's seat.

NOTES

Ash Crosses Spell

REQUIREMENTS:

❄ Wood ashes

INSTRUCTIONS:

Collect cold wood ashes from a previous fire.

Cast a protective circle around the area where you will perform the spell.

Use the ashes to draw equal-armed crosses on the ground, sidewalk, or porch. Visualize the crosses as barriers of protection.

As you create each ash cross, recite the following incantation:

Ashes to ashes, I call on the Four,
Protect us from harm, guard our door.

Stand back and visualize the protective energy radiating from the ash crosses, forming a barrier around your space.

By the power of these sacred ashes, protection is granted, and harm is kept at bay.

NOTES

Bottle of Threads

By creating a protective bottle. this spell helps fight off bad influences and negative energy. By filling a bottle with colorful threads and chanting an incantation, you create a powerful talisman of protection.

REQUIREMENTS:

❁ A large bottle
❁ Small pieces of thread in various colors (excluding black)

INSTRUCTIONS:

Arrange your tools and ingredients on a small table or altar.

Begin by adding each piece of thread into the bottle, one at a time. As you place each thread, chant with intent:

"Tangle the bane, twist and bind,
Protect this space, body, and mind."

Repeat this process, adding thread by thread, until the bottle is full. With each addition, chant:

"Tangle the bane, twist and bind,
Shield this space, with threads entwined."

Once the bottle is full, cap it securely. Place it in a window, in the attic, or in a cupboard where it will not be disturbed.

Take a moment to sense the protective energy radiating from the bottle, knowing that it is warding off any negative forces.

Candle of Protection

Keep the candle and burn it during meditation whenever you feel the need for extra protection. When the candle is completely burned, you may repeat this spell if necessary.

REQUIREMENTS:

❁ One orange candle
❁ One carnation flower
❁ Fresh basil leaves
❁ Consecrated water

MOON PHASE:
Full Moon

INSTRUCTIONS:

Begin your ritual in your preferred manner, casting your sacred circle.

Setup the Altar:

Place the carnation flower in a bowl of consecrated water.

Set the basil in front of the orange candle.

Light the orange candle with the Presence candle.

Breathe deeply, clear your mind, and focus on the intention of protection.

Close your eyes and concentrate on the protective powers. Visualize a strong, glowing shell surrounding you, emanating heat and light. In a powerful voice, chant:

"Guardians and deities, heed my call,
With the power of the Lord and Lady all.
Encircle me now in fire's warm glow,
Grounded by earth's enduring flow.
Winds bring change, waters soothe,
Energy flows, protection to smooth.
In this shield I trust, my fears released,
Connected to life's pulse, my soul is at peace.
For the good of all, I cast this spell,
May protection surround, keeping me well."

Let the candle burn for as long as you desire. Use this time to meditate, envisioning the spell taking form and releasing into the cosmos. When you are ready, snuff out the candle.

Perform the wine and cake blessing, consuming them to ground the energy.

Dismiss the elements and any spirits present.

Close the circle.

Take the basil leaves and scatter them on the ground under the light of the full moon, completing the spell.

Keep the candle and burn it during meditation whenever you feel the need for extra protection.

NOTES

Circle of Protection

It is also an ideal option to cast when a protective spell asks to cast a circle.

REQUIREMENTS:

❀ Athame or wand for casting the circle

INSTRUCTIONS:

Begin in the East.

Hold your athame or wand and draw a circle, moving deosil (clockwise), and chant:

> "I, [Your Name], conjure thee, O circle of might,
> Encircle every tower in the radiant light.
> Be thou a place of truth, joy, and love,
> Encircling flight of eagle, hawk, and dove.
> Mighty shield of Lady and Lord,
> Rampart of thought, action, and word.
> To work in peace, powerful and free,
> Those who walk between worlds, I conjure thee.
> A boundary to protect, concentrate, and contain,
> That power raised here shall not be in vain.
> Wherefore do I bless and consecrate thee,
> In the names of Lady Gaia and Lord Pan, so let it be."

Take a moment to sense and absorb all of the protective conjured energies around you.

Continue with the Invocation.

Invocation of the Deities:

"The sacred circle now surrounds us.
We gather here in peace and love thus.
We invite the God and Goddess, Lord and Lady,
Father and Mother of all life, to aid us steadily.
Guard us within this circle's embrace,
From all evil and harm, in every space.
In all things, as our will is spun,
By Lady Gaia and Lord Pan, our protection is done."

Your circle is now cast, and protection is in place. May the deities guard you and keep you safe in your magical workings.

NOTES

Danger, Away! Charm

This simple charm is intended to keep you safe when you feel threatened or in danger. You can make a portable talisman that protects you from harm by packing a small jar full of potent protecting herbs.

REQUIREMENTS:

❀ 1 small jar (portable size)
❀ Fennel seeds
❀ Marigold petals
❀ Bay leaves
❀ Nutmeg
❀ Mustard seeds

INSTRUCTIONS:

Find a quiet and undisturbed place where you can perform this spell without interruptions. Arrange your tools and ingredients on a small table or altar.

Begin by adding each ingredient to the small jar, one by one. As you add each herb, chant with intent:

"Fennel seeds, protection bring,
Guard me well with shielded ring."

Add marigold petals and chant:

"Marigold, with golden light,
Keep me safe both day and night."

Add the bay leaves and chant:

> "Bay leaves strong, ward off fear,
> Protect me when danger is near."

Add the nutmeg and chant:

> "Nutmeg warm, with strength imbue,
> Keep me safe in all I do."

Add the mustard seeds and chant:

> "Mustard seeds, so small yet bold,
> Guard me with your power untold."

Take a moment to sense the protective energy emanating from the charm. Trust that it will guard you in times of need.

Whenever you feel threatened, hold the jar and inhale deeply. Visualize the protective energy surrounding you. Chant:

> "Herbs of power, strong and true,
> Protect me now, in all I do."

NOTES

Dark Moon Protection Chant

This protective incantation aims to summon the influence of the black moon and the Lady Crone to restore balance and safeguard against negative energy. Chanting the incantation beneath the dark moon invokes its ability to safeguard and equilibrate the energies surrounding you.

REQUIREMENTS

❀ The presence of the dark moon

INSTRUCTIONS:

Find a quiet and undisturbed place where you can perform this chant without interruptions. Ensure you are outdoors or near a window where you can see the dark moon.

Stand under the dark moon and focus your intent on invoking the Lady Crone's power.

With clear intent and focus, chant:

> "Dark moon, Lady Crone so wise,
> By Your power, hear my cries.
> Send what's due, set things aright,
> Protect me now, with Your might.
> No harm I wish, just peace to find,
> Shield me from energies unkind."

Take a moment to sense the protective energy of the dark moon surrounding you. Trust that it will shield you from any negative forces.

NOTES

Divine Elements Protection Charm

Using the strength of the Goddess and the God, this protection charm is intended to keep you safe. A potent talisman that guards and defends is created by consecration of a symbol with fire and air.

REQUIREMENTS:

❀ One red candle
❀ One white candle
❀ A small piece of white paper
❀ Oil (such as olive or almond oil)
❀ Ink pen

INSTRUCTIONS:

Find a quiet and undisturbed place to perform the spell. Arrange your tools and ingredients on a small table or altar.

Set the white candle alight on the left to represent the Goddess and the red candle on the right to represent the God. Place the materials for the spell between the two candles.

Using the oil and your right index finger, draw a pentacle (a star within a circle) in the middle of the white paper. As you do, chant:

> "With the seal of this pentagram,
> Protection charm, by my hand."

Using the pen, draw your personal symbol for protection in the center of the oil-drawn pentacle. Chant:

> "With this rune, I call to thee,
> Protect and guard, this charm for me."

Roll the paper tightly lengthwise and bind it with the red ribbon. Hold the charm over the flame of the red candle. Chant:

"I consecrate myself in fire,
To protect and guard, my true desire."

Pass the charm through the smoke of the white candle, consecrating it in the name of air. Chant:

"By the smoke of air, pure and bright,
Protect this charm, both day and night."

Seal the left end of the charm with white wax and the right end with red wax, completing the ritual.

Hold the charm with both hands, focusing on its purpose and visualizing it as a powerful shield.

Take a moment to sense the protective energy imbued within the charm. Trust that it will guard you from harm.

NOTES

Divine Protection

REQUIREMENTS:

❁ A white candle
❁ A piece of paper and pen
❁ A small bowl of water
❁ A handful of salt

INSTRUCTIONS:

Find a quiet and undisturbed place in your home. Arrange your white candle, paper, pen, bowl of water, and salt on a small table or altar.

Cast a circle if you wish.

Light the white candle, focusing on its flame as a beacon of protection and divine energy.

Write your name on the piece of paper. Hold the paper in your hands and chant:

> "God and Goddess of the skies,
> Hear and respond to my cries.
> Lift me up in your embrace,
> Away from harm, grant me grace."

Sprinkle a pinch of salt into the bowl of water, stirring it gently. Dip your fingers into the mixture and touch it to your forehead, chanting:

> "Shield me from the rage I face,
> Help me find a peaceful place.
> Grant me strength in all I do,
> Keep my heart steadfast and true."

Hold the paper over the candle's flame, but do not let it catch fire. Visualize a circle of light around you filled with love and protection. Chant:

"Let those I love return my care,
Each day teach me to be aware.
Keep my spirit, day and night,
Guide me with your gentle light."

Fold the paper and place it under the candle. Let the candle burn for a while, then extinguish it, knowing the spell is sealed.

Close the circle if you cast one, and take a moment to feel the divine protection surrounding you.

NOTES

Dragon's Light Protection

This potent protective incantation invokes the might and guardianship of the dragon's luminescence. By harnessing the dragon's power, you can establish a protective barrier around yourself and your environment, guaranteeing safety and tranquilly.

REQUIREMENTS:

❀ A dragon figurine or image
❀ One red candle
❀ One white candle
❀ A piece of paper and pen
❀ A quiet, undisturbed space

INSTRUCTIONS:

Find a quiet and undisturbed place where you can perform this ritual without interruptions. Arrange your tools on a small table or altar.

Place the red candle on your left and the white candle on your right. Place the dragon figurine or image between the two candles.

On the piece of paper, write the current month. This helps to anchor the spell in the present time and enhance its power.

Light the red candle, symbolizing the dragon's fiery strength, and then the white candle, symbolizing purity and protection.

Hold the dragon figurine or look at the image, and with the piece of paper in front of you, chant the following incantation with focus and intent:

"On this night of [current month], by dragon's light,
I call to thee, grant me thy might.
By the power of three, I summon thee,
Guard all around me, so mote it be!"

As you chant, visualize a powerful dragon's light forming a protective shield around you and your space. See this light as impenetrable, glowing with the strength of the dragon.

Place the piece of paper with the written month under the dragon figurine or image, solidifying the spell's connection to the present.

NOTES

Driving Charm for Safe Travels

This driving charm is intended to safeguard you whilst driving, promoting clarity, rapid reactions, and comprehensive safety. By amalgamating these protecting components and envisioning a secure voyage, one can forge a potent talisman for their vehicle.

REQUIREMENTS:

✿ Three holly leaves
✿ One clove of garlic
✿ One sprig of cedar
✿ One piece of clear quartz
✿ One piece of dragon's blood resin
✿ A small box

INSTRUCTIONS:

Find a quiet and undisturbed place where you can prepare this charm without interruptions. Arrange your tools and ingredients on a small table or altar.

Place the three holly leaves, one clove of garlic, one sprig of cedar, one piece of clear quartz, and one piece of dragon's blood resin into the small box. As you add each item, focus on its protective qualities and visualize it contributing to your safety.

Hold the box shut and close your eyes.

Imagine yourself driving your car, surrounded by a protective shield of light. Visualize yourself being clear-minded, keen, and observant. See yourself making quick and accurate decisions, reacting with split-second timing, and feeling joy in your role as a safe driver.

While holding the box and maintaining your visualization, chant the following incantation three times:

"Holly, garlic, cedar, quartz, and dragon's blood,
Protect me on the open road,
Keep my mind clear and sharp as a blade,
Guide my hands with swift, safe aid.
In this charm, I trust and believe,
Safe travels always, I receive."

Once you feel the energy of the spell is strong and clear, place the box in the glove compartment of your car, securing its protective presence within your vehicle.

If you ever feel the need, you can periodically take out the box, hold it, and repeat the visualization and incantation to reinforce its power.

NOTES

Herbal Protection Mojo

A protective sachet to safeguard your house and everyone who lives there. You can construct a magical guardian for your home by binding the herbs with a red string and calling forth their power.

REQUIREMENTS:

❀ 7″ square of cotton
❀ Basil
❀ Fennel
❀ Dill
❀ Red string
❀ Athame

INSTRUCTIONS:

Find a quiet and undisturbed place where you can perform this spell without interruptions. Arrange your ingredients and tools on a small table or altar.

Place the basil, fennel, and dill in the center of the 7″ square of cotton. Tie the cloth up with the red string, securing the herbs inside.

Begin tying the red string into knots. With the first knot, chant:

"I bind thee to protect this space,
Guard all who dwell within this place."

Continue tying the string into a total of 13 knots, repeating the line with each knot.

Pick up your athame with your dominant hand, face north, and gently poke the sachet with the tip of the athame. Chant:

"May this charm, by my hands made,
Serve as guardian, lend me aid.
Protector of this home, stand tall,
Shield all within these walls."

Place the sachet in the highest part of your home, ensuring it is securely hung.

Take a moment to sense the protective energy surrounding your home.

Trust that the sachet will guard your household from harm.

NOTES

Herbal Protection Mojo 2

REQUIREMENTS:

❁ A piece of white cotton cloth (7-inch square)
❁ Three protective herbs (choose from: basil, dill, fennel, St. John's Wort, rosemary, tarragon, horehound, vervain)
❁ Earthenware bowl
❁ Red yarn (7 inches long)
❁ Athame (ritual knife)

INSTRUCTIONS:

Cut a 7-inch square piece of white cotton cloth. The number seven is significant in magic, so be precise.

Choose three protective herbs from the list. No substitutions in number—three is key. Place a small amount of each in an earthenware bowl.

Gently mix the herbs in the bowl, humming a protective tune if you like. Ensure you're using a non-plastic, non-aluminum bowl.

Lay the cloth on your altar. Place the mixed herbs in the center of the cloth. Pull up the four corners to form a pouch.

Use a 7-inch piece of red yarn to tie the pouch. Tie the first knot while chanting:

"I bind thee to protect this house and all within it!"

Repeat this chant with each knot, tying a total of thirteen knots.

Hold the sachet in your non-dominant hand and your athame in your dominant hand. Face North and gently poke the sachet with your athame.

Declare with conviction:

"By my will and with my hands,
This charm shall guard and protect these lands.
Protector and Guardian, here I decree,
From this moment forth, so shall it be!"

Hang the sachet in the highest part of your house using the red yarn. This will ensure it watches over and protects your home.

Your herbal protection mojo is now complete. The sachet will serve as a guardian, ensuring the safety and well-being of all who reside within your home.

NOTES

Home and Personal Protection Spell for Renters

This spell is designed to shield you and your rental property from any evil energy or spells that might be directed at you. You may make sure that any negative energy is sent back to its origin by using the law of three.

INSTRUCTIONS:

Find a peaceful area within your home where you can perform the spell without interruptions.

Close your eyes, take a few deep breaths, and visualize a protective barrier surrounding your home.

Stand in the center of your home, feeling grounded and centered.

With conviction, recite the following spell:

> "Any spell cast against this place,
> Or the tenant of this space,
> Be scattered now, be gone, depart,
> Return to sender, swift and smart.
> By the law of three, let it be,
> My will is strong, protected be. "

As you chant, visualize a shimmering shield of light enveloping your entire home, repelling any negative energies or intentions.

House Guardians

REQUIREMENTS:

❀ Representations of your guardians (pictures, statues, crafts, etc.)
❀ A cleansed white candle for each guardian
❀ Sage smudge stick or cleansing incense (like sandalwood or raw sage)
❀ A bowl to catch ashes
❀ Protection amulets (optional)
❀ A bell (optional)

INSTRUCTIONS:

Pick a representation for every entrance in your home, whether it be a statue, picture, or handcrafted object that holds special importance for you, and make sure it is consecrated and prepared for usage.

Before summoning the guardians, cleanse your home thoroughly. Light the sage smudge stick, holding a bowl to catch the ashes. Starting at the front door, walk clockwise around your home. Chant:

"As I walk through every room,
Let this house be cleansed of gloom.
With sacred smoke and purifying light,
Negative energies take their flight."

Move the smudge stick in a counterclockwise circle or a straight line towards the walls. Visualize negative energy flowing out. At each window, trace bars with the smudge stick, chanting:

"I bar this portal from allowing harm.
Only peace may enter, with this charm."

For outside doors, draw a circle around the doorframe three times, saying:

"No negative energies may enter here,
May all who come bring love and cheer.
If a negative person approaches near,
May they leave their troubles, have no fear."

Continue through all rooms, including attics and basements, if accessible. End back at the front door, concluding with:

"This house is cleansed, pure, and bright,
Blessed with love and protective light."

Bring your guardian representations and candles to the place where your family spends the most time together, such as the dining room or living room. Place a candle before each guardian representation.

Light the first candle, focusing on the door you wish the guardian to protect. Hold the representation and chant:

"Spirit of the ancient ways,
Come forth now and guard these days.
Protect this home, both night and day,
Shield us from harm in every way."

Repeat this process for each guardian, assigning them to their respective doors. Meditate briefly with the guardians, envisioning them standing vigil at each entrance. Place the representations in their designated positions around the house and extinguish the candles. These candles are reserved for summoning the guardians.

ADDITIONAL INFORMATION

Light the guardian candles and call them again in the place where they were originally summoned. Introduce each family member, including pets, to the guardians. If someone does not wish to participate, explain to the guardians that they also belong in the house and should be protected. Chant:

"Guardians wise, protect us all,
From the eldest member to the small.
Those who choose not to take part,
Shield them still with all your heart."

Meditate with your guardians regularly. Light the candles, call them, and spend time communicating with them. Offer your gratitude and seek their guidance. On special occasions, such as May Day, honor them with additional offerings or rituals.

Always inform your guardians of any significant changes in the household, such as expecting a child, getting a new pet, redecorating, or hosting a party. This ensures they are aware and can adjust their protection as needed. To do this, chant:

"Guardians strong, guardians dear,
We have news for you to hear.
Changes come, and we respect,
Your vigilant watch and your effect."

Leave offerings for your guardians when you call them, when they've done something good for you, and during Sabbats and Esbats. A small dish of leftover food and drink from dinner placed where pets and children cannot reach is ideal. By morning, the essence of the food will be consumed. Chant:

"To you, our guardians, we give thanks,
For your protection, steadfast ranks.
This food and drink we offer now,
In gratitude, we make this vow."

Your guardians are now in place, offering their protection and guidance. May your home be a sanctuary of peace and safety. Blessed be your home and all who dwell within.

If you move, inform your guardians that their services are no longer needed and thank them for their protection. Chant:

"Guardians who have served so true,
We offer heartfelt thanks to you.
Our journey takes us to new land,
We release you now with open hand."

House Protection Spell Jar

The purpose of this spell is to shield your house from damage and bad energy. You can construct a magical barrier that protects everyone in your home by combining the protective qualities of nine ancient herbs.

REQUIREMENTS:

❀ 1 glass bottle or jar with a cap
❀ A mixing bowl
❀ A funnel (you can make one with a rolled-up piece of paper)
❀ 9 herbs of your choice from the list below:

Herb List: Acacia, Aloe, Angelica, Anise, Ash, Basil, Birch, Blackberry, Blueberry, Broom, Caraway, Carnation, Cedar, Cinquefoil, Clover, Cotton, Cypress, Dill, Eucalyptus, Fennel, Flax, Foxglove, Grass, Hazel, Heather, Holly, Irish Moss, Ivy, Lilac, Mandrake, Marigold, Mistletoe, Mugwort, Mulberry, Oak, Olive, Pine, Primrose, Raspberry, Rice, Rose, Rosemary, Sandalwood, Spanish Moss, Thistle, Valerian, Violet, Willow

INSTRUCTIONS:

Find a quiet and undisturbed place where you can perform this spell without interruptions. Arrange your tools and ingredients on a small table or altar.

Choose nine herbs from the provided list that resonate with you and your intent for protection.

Pour each selected herb into the mixing bowl one by one. As you add each herb, chant:

"_____ that protects, protect my home and all within."

Using your hands, mix the herbs together in the bowl. As you mix, visualize your home being enveloped in a safe and secure aura.

Use the funnel to pour the mixed herbs into the glass bottle or jar. Seal it tightly with the cap.

Bury the bottle outside, in front of your front step. If you live in an apartment or a place where burying is not possible, hide the jar somewhere near your doorway but out of view.

Take a moment to visualize the protective energy radiating from the bottle, forming a barrier around your home.

Reinforce as Needed: If you feel the need to reinforce the protection, revisit the spell and add more herbs to the jar, repeating the chants.

NOTES

Incense for Protecting the House from Evil

REQUIREMENTS:

❀ 4 ounces Valerian root
❀ 2 ounces Rue
❀ 2 ounces Bay leaves
❀ 3 tablespoons Dill
❀ 2 ounces Caraway seeds
❀ 4 parts Lavender
❀ 6 teaspoons Sandalwood

INSTRUCTIONS:

Begin by creating a sacred space in your home where you can mix and bless the ingredients. Light a white candle and cast a circle if you wish.

In a large bowl, combine the Valerian root, Rue, Bay leaves, Dill, Caraway seeds, Lavender, and Sandalwood. As you add each ingredient, chant:

"Valerian, Rue, and Bay,
Keep all evil far away.
Dill, Caraway, Lavender's bloom,
Protect and cleanse every room.
Sandalwood's sacred power,
Guard this home at every hour."

Using your hands, mix the ingredients thoroughly, visualizing a protective light surrounding your home. Feel the energy of each herb combining to form a powerful shield.

Hold the bowl of mixed incense up to the candle flame and say:

"By fire's light and herb's embrace,
Protect this home, sacred space.
Let no darkness linger here,
Shield us from all harm and fear."

Using the Incense

Place a small amount of the incense on a charcoal disc in a heatproof dish. Allow the smoke to fill your home, walking through each room to ensure the protective energy reaches every corner.

As you move through your home, repeat the following incantation:

"Smoke of herbs, strong and pure,
Guard this home, make it secure.
Evil be gone, leave this place,
Protect us with your sacred grace."

Extinguish the candle and close the circle if you cast one. Take a moment to feel the calm and protection surrounding your home.

Once you have finished, store the remaining incense in a glass jar with a tight lid. Keep it in a cool, dark place, and use as needed to maintain the protective barrier.

NOTES

Incense to Ward Off and Protect Against Ghosts

REQUIREMENTS:

✤ 3 ounces Juniper Leaves
✤ 4 tablespoons Dried Rosemary
✤ 2 ounces Fennel Seeds
✤ 2 teaspoons Basil
✤ 3 teaspoons Linden Flowers
✤ 2 teaspoons Angelica
✤ Pinch of Salt

INSTRUCTIONS:

Begin by creating a sacred space in your home. Light a white candle and cast a protective circle if you wish.

In a large bowl, combine the Juniper leaves, Dried Rosemary, Fennel seeds, Basil, Linden flowers, Angelica, and a pinch of Salt. As you add each ingredient, chant:

"Juniper, Rosemary, Fennel bright,
Keep away spirits in the night.
Basil, Linden, Angelica pure,
Protect this home, make it secure.
Salt of Earth, strong and bold,
Ward off ghosts, both young and old."

Mix the ingredients thoroughly with your hands, visualizing a protective barrier forming around your home. Feel the energy of each herb enhancing this shield.

Hold the bowl of mixed incense up to the candle flame and say:

"By fire's light and herb's embrace,
Ghosts and spirits, leave this place.
None shall enter, none shall stay,
Protect this home, both night and day."

Using the Incense

Place a small amount of the incense on a charcoal disc in a heatproof dish. Allow the smoke to fill your home, walking through each room to ensure the protective energy reaches every corner.

As you move through your home, repeat the following incantation:

"Smoke of herbs, rise and twine,
Keep all spirits from this shrine.
Ghosts begone, leave this space,
Protect us with your sacred grace."

Extinguish the candle and close the circle if you cast one. Take a moment to feel the peace and protection surrounding your home.

Once you have finished, store the remaining incense in a glass jar with a tight lid. Keep it in a cool, dark place, and use as needed to maintain the protective barrier.

NOTES

Italian Car Charm

REQUIREMENTS:

❀ Salt
❀ Piece of palm leaf
❀ Tiny gold horn
❀ Small pair of scissors or a small knife
❀ White cloth
❀ Red ribbon
❀ Protective oil

INSTRUCTIONS:

Cast a protective circle around your working area to focus your energy and keep out distractions.

Lay out a piece of white cloth.

Place a pinch of salt, a piece of palm leaf, a tiny gold horn, and a small pair of scissors or knife in the center of the cloth.

Gather the corners of the cloth together, forming a small pouch with the items inside.

Secure the pouch tightly with a red ribbon, tying it in a firm knot.

Hold the pouch in your hands, close your eyes, and visualize a protective light surrounding it.

Chant the following incantation:

> Salt and palm, horn and knife,
> Guard this car and protect its life.
> In white cloth bound with ribbon red,
> Keep us safe, wherever we're led.

Feel your energy flowing into the charm, imbuing it with protective magic.

Place the charm in the glove compartment of your car for ongoing protection.

Dab a small amount of protective oil on the seat belts of your car.

As you apply the oil, say:

Oil of safety, pure and true,
Guard us well in all we do.
Secure us firmly, keep us tight,
Protect us both day and night.

NOTES

Knight Protective Invocation

REQUIREMENTS:

❃ An athame or wand

INSTRUCTIONS:

Draw a circle on the ground, ensuring all casters enter. The more casters, the stronger the spell.

Hold your athame or wand high and chant:

> "Hear me, knights of times gone by,
> Guardians of the ancient law, drawn nigh.
> Hear me, knights of English tongue,
> Whose valiant deeds remain unsung.
> Hear me, warriors fallen in fight,
> Whose blades brought forth the morning light.
> Hear me, knights of olden days,
> Hear me, spirits in the haze."

Summoning the Spirits:

> "This night, I summon thee to stand,
> Lend me your strength, your guiding hand.
> Though bodies fade, your spirits bright,
> I call you forth into the night.
> By spirit blade, by might so true,
> By ancient oaths, I summon you."

Enlisting the Knights:

"Come forth, knights of battles past,
A new cause beckons, a spell is cast.
Each of thee, I call by name,
Join my cause, protect my claim.
Stand with me, guard my side,
Shield me from the spirits' tide.
Protect me from harm, both near and far,
Fight my battles, wherever they are."

Reinforcement and Closure:

"Hear me, spirits of valiant knights,
Come to my aid, stand in my light.
Protect me from spirits' harm and dread,
Shield me from forces that I may tread.
I invoke you, I summon you, stand by me,
With your strength, so shall it be."

Activating the Army:

"Let this army now be formed,
By your spirits, I am warmed.
This spell is cast, the circle complete,
With knights' protection, I shall not retreat."

NOTES

Magic Bath
for Protection and Purification

The purpose of this enchanted bath ritual is to cleanse and protect by eliminating harmful influences and energies. You may make a bath that protects and revitalises your soul by steeping basil, a potent herb for purification and protection.

REQUIREMENTS:

- 1 teaspoon of dried basil
- 1 cup of boiling water
- A strainer
- A bathtub

INSTRUCTIONS:

Find a quiet and undisturbed place where you can prepare and take your bath without interruptions.

Pour 1 cup of boiling water over 1 teaspoon of dried basil. Allow it to steep for a few minutes, infusing the water with its protective and cleansing properties.

Use a strainer to remove the basil leaves, ensuring only the infused water is added to your bath.

Draw a warm bath and add the basil-infused water. As you pour the infusion into the bath, visualize the water glowing with a protective light.

Step into the bath and immerse yourself fully. Feel the warmth of the water enveloping you, carrying away all negativity and stress.

As you soak, chant the following incantation to enhance the protective and purifying effects:

"Basil green, so pure and bright,
Cleanse my spirit, day and night.
Wash away the dark, the cold,
Protect my heart, my mind, my soul.
Negative thoughts, be gone from me,
In this sacred bath, I am free."

Close your eyes and visualize the water drawing out all negative energies and influences. See the water around you shimmering with a protective aura, creating a barrier against harm.

Remain in the bath for as long as you feel necessary, absorbing the protective and cleansing energies.

When you are ready, drain the bathwater, envisioning all negativity being washed away with it.

Step out of the bath feeling refreshed, purified, and shielded from negative influences.

NOTES

Magic Chant of Protection

This magical chant calls upon the Goddess to grant you protection from the outside world, to shield you from harm and to bring peace to your soul. By reciting this chant with heartfelt intent, you invoke the divine energy to safeguard you and soothe your spirit.

INSTRUCTIONS:

Find a quiet and undisturbed place where you can perform this spell without interruptions. Arrange your tools (if any) on a small table or altar.

Stand or sit comfortably, close your eyes, and take a few deep breaths. Visualize a protective light surrounding you.

With your heart open and your mind focused, recite the following chant:

"Goddess, grant me your shield, so strong,
Protect me from the world's harsh throng.
Words that wound, let them not sting,
Fears that haunt, peace let them bring.
Mixed emotions, set them free,
Harm to none, release in me.
Goddess, you know my pain so deep,
I am your child, my soul you keep.
I seek a dream to ease my plight,
Soothe my soul through day and night.
Grant me your protection, ever near,
Keep me safe, away from fear."

As you chant, visualize the protective light becoming stronger, forming a barrier that shields you from negativity and harm.

Take a moment to bask in the protective energy surrounding you. Trust that the Goddess's shield will guard you from harm and bring peace to your soul.t

70

Magic Cone of Protection

This spell deflects any bad ideas or energies by enveloping you in a strong cone of protective energy. You can create a shield that protects your wellbeing by meditating and imagining a protective vortex.

INSTRUCTIONS:

Find a quiet place where you will not be disturbed.

Sit comfortably in the centre of your protected circle.

Close your eyes and take deep calming breaths, grounding yourself.

Focus on your intention to create a protective cone of energy.

Imagine an electric blue light forming around the room, swirling like a vortex.

As it moves towards you, see the light transforming into a bright white and then into a shimmering silver.

Visualize this gelatinous silver light surrounding you completely, creating a reflective barrier.

Say the following chant to empower the protective cone:

> "Cone of light, electric blue,
> Swirl around, protect me true.
> Turn to silver, strong and bright,
> Shield me now, both day and night."

Feel the protective energy solidify around you, deflecting any negative thoughts or forms that come your way.

Spend a few minutes meditating within this cone, reinforcing its power.

Mirror Protection from Negative Energies

REQUIREMENTS:

❀ 1 black candle
❀ Caraway seeds
❀ A small mirror

INSTRUCTIONS:

Find a quiet and undisturbed place where you can cast your circle and perform the spell. Arrange your ingredients and tools on a small table or altar.

Cast a protective circle around your sacred space to create a barrier between you and any external energies.

Light the black candle, focusing on its flame. This candle will absorb negative energies and act as a protective beacon.

Carefully sprinkle caraway seeds onto the candle's flame and over the surface of the mirror. Visualize the seeds empowering your protective shield.

Close your eyes and imagine yourself surrounded by a glowing, magical shield. See negative energies bouncing off this shield and returning to their source.

Open your eyes and stand facing North. Hold the mirror in front of you with the reflective side pointing outward. Chant:

"Mirror bright, protection clear,
Reflect all harm, send it far from here.
May the energy return to its source,
Causing no harm along its course."

Turn to the East and repeat the chant, invoking the element of Air. Turn

South for Fire, and West for Water, repeating the chant each time.

Once you have completed the invocation for all directions, close the circle to seal the protective energy.

Take a moment to sense the protective energy surrounding you. Trust that your magical shield will guard you from negative influences.

NOTES

Mirror Spell
for Protecting Your Home

REQUIREMENTS:

❀ Censer
❀ Image of the Goddess
❀ 12-inch round mirror
❀ 9 white candles
❀ Frankincense, copal, or rosemary

INSTRUCTIONS:

Place the censer in the center of the altar before the image of the Goddess.

Arrange the 9 white candles in a circle around the altar.

Light the incense in the censer, allowing its smoke to purify the space.

Begin with the candle directly in front of the Goddess image.

As you light each candle, say:

"Luna Beam, protect my Gleam."

Hold the mirror up high and call upon the Goddess in her lunar aspect with the following chant:

"O Great Goddess of lunar gleam,
Mistress of the sea's bright beam,
Guardian of the mystic night,
Keeper of the sacred sight;
In this circle of candle's shine,
With your mirror's magic divine,
Shield this home from harm and bane,
Let no ill or woe remain! "

74

Stand before the altar, holding the mirror to reflect the candle flames.

Slowly move counterclockwise around the circle, allowing the reflected light to cast away negativity.

Gradually increase your speed, envisioning the light burning away all ill vibrations.

Continue until you feel a shift in the atmosphere, sensing that your home is cleansed and protected by the Goddess.

Return to the altar and face the image of the Goddess.

Offer your thanks to the Goddess for her protection.

Pinch out each candle one by one, binding them together with a white cord.

Store the candles in a safe place for future use if needed.

Your home is now blessed and shielded by the Goddess's mighty power. May it remain a sanctuary of peace and light.

NOTES

Object Enchantment for its Protection

This potent incantation is intended to safeguard a valued item from undesired contact or damage. By delineating a pentagram with enchanted luminescence and reciting a protective spell, you establish a shield that safeguards the object continuously.

REQUIREMENTS:

✷ The object to be protected

INSTRUCTIONS:

Find a quiet and undisturbed place where you can perform this spell without interruptions. Arrange the object to be protected on a small table or altar.

Close your eyes and visualize a radiant light flowing from your fingertip, ready to be directed.

With your finger, trace a pentagram over the object. As you do, chant with intent:

"With the pentacle I lay,
Protection here by night and day.
Those who may not touch, beware,
Let their fingers burn in snare."

Strengthen the protection by invoking the Law of Three. Chant:

"By the rule of three, I decree,
This is my will, protected be."

As you chant, envision three separate circles of light forming around the object, each adding to the protective barrier.

Take a moment to sense the protective energy surrounding the object. Trust that it is now shielded from harm.

Onion and Garlic Protection Charm

This potent charm wards off evil spirits and negative influences from your household, ensuring the safety and well-being of your family. Renew this charm annually to maintain its protective power.

REQUIREMENTS:

✿ 3 onions with leaves attached
✿ 3 garlic bulbs with leaves attached

INSTRUCTIONS:

Arrange the onions and garlic bulbs together, aligning their leaves.

Begin braiding the leaves of the onions and garlic together, intertwining them carefully.

As you braid, visualize a protective barrier forming around your home, shielding it from all harm.

As you braid, chant the following incantation to infuse the charm with protective energy:

"Bulbs of power, layered tight,
Guard us from all harm and spite.
By leaf and root, protect this space,
Keep all evil from this place."

Once braided, hang the charm in your kitchen or another central area of your home.

Envision a dome of light forming around your home, impenetrable by malevolent spirits.

To provide continuous protection, replace the charm once a year. This straightforward yet effective charm will protect your family from bad spirits' meddling and establish a peaceful haven in your house.

Planetary Shield

Every night, the jars will absorb the planetary energies, fortifying the barrier that protects your family and house. Have patience and let the magic develop. The protection will be stronger the longer the jars are left undisturbed.

REQUIREMENTS:

❁ 11 small jars
❁ Permanent marker
❁ Barley
❁ Sage
❁ Garlic
❁ Parsley
❁ Rosemary
❁ Ailanthus
❁ Rose petals
❁ Seaweed or any water plant
❁ Silverweed
❁ Weeping Willow
❁ Moonwort

INSTRUCTIONS:

Using the permanent marker, label each jar with the name of a planet, including Earth, Moon, and Sun.

Draw the corresponding symbols of each celestial body on the jars.

Fill each jar halfway with warm water.

Sun jar: Add rosemary.
Mercury jar: Add parsley.
Venus jar: Add rose petals.
Earth jar: Add barley.
Mars jar: Add garlic.

Jupiter jar: Add sage.
Saturn jar: Add weeping willow.
Uranus jar: Add ailanthus.
Neptune jar: Add water plant.
Pluto jar: Add silverweed.
Moon jar Add moonwort.

Close each jar tightly.

Arrange the jars in a straight row and chant:

"I invoke the gods of these celestial spheres,
Apollo, Hermes, Aphrodite, Gaia,
Diana, Ares, Zeus, Uranus,
Saturn, Poseidon, Hades, hear us.
Grant your power, protection's might,
Shield us now, day and night."

Visualize each planet's energy infusing the jars, creating a powerful protective shield around your home.

Chant:

"Guardians of the celestial heights,
Protect our home, both day and night.
By the planets' power and their might,
Shield us well, within your light."

Let the jars sit out under the night sky.

The next day, bury the jars in your yard or garden, close to your home. If this is not possible, store them in the back of a closet or a seldom-used cabinet.

Potpourri Protection from Bad Luck

REQUIREMENTS:

❀ 1/2 cup juniper berries (whole)
❀ 1/2 cup basil (whole)
❀ 2 tablespoons frankincense (ground)
❀ 2 tablespoons dill seeds
❀ 2 tablespoons cloves (whole)
❀ 8 bay leaves (torn into pieces)

INSTRUCTIONS:

Collect all the listed ingredients and place them in a bowl.

With your hands, gently mix the juniper berries, basil, frankincense, dill seeds, cloves, and torn bay leaves. As you blend them, visualize a shield of positive energy surrounding you and your home.

Focus your intentions on protection and the dispelling of bad luck. Channel your positive energies into the mixture, infusing it with your power.

Place the mixed ingredients into a potpourri pot or a non-metallic bowl.

As you place the potpourri in the chosen container, chant softly:

"Berries and basil, frankincense bright,
Cloves and dill, bay leaves take flight.
Ward off bad luck, misfortune dispel,
Bring good fortune, where we dwell."

Place the potpourri in a central location in your home, such as the living room or near the entrance. This will allow the protective energies to radiate throughout your space.

Replace the potpourri every month or as needed to maintain its protective potency. Discard the old potpourri respectfully, returning it to the earth if possible.

NOTES

Protect Your Abode While Traveling

While you are away, this spell makes sure your house is safe. You can protect your home from theft and bad energy by enchantment of keys and basic precautions.

REQUIREMENTS:

❀ A key for each door in your house
❀ Red ribbon
❀ A broom
❀ A blue candle (optional for traveling)
❀ A small mirror

INSTRUCTIONS:

Find a quiet and undisturbed place in your home to gather your ingredients and focus your intent.

Collect a key for each door in your house.

Move slowly through your home. At each door, touch the key to the door and chant:

> "Lock out thieves in the night,
> Lock out thieves in the light,
> Lock out thieves out of sight."

Visualize a protective barrier forming as you say these words. Repeat until each key has touched each door.

Once all the doors are touched, tie the keys together with the red ribbon and hang them over the front door. This will serve as a talisman to ward off thieves.

Before you leave, clean your bed and place a broom in it with the bristles on the pillow. This will deter negative energy from settling in your absence.

Place a small mirror on the headboard of your bed or facing the door. This will repel negative influences and keep you safe throughout the night.

Take a moment to sense the protective energy surrounding your home and yourself. Trust that the spell will guard your abode and ensure your safety.

Repeat this spell each time you travel to ensure ongoing protection.

NOTES

Protection Brew

This potent brew is designed to ward off evil and protect your home from negative energies. It is used to anoint windows and doors, and sprinkled at the four corners of your house to create a protective barrier.

REQUIREMENTS:

✤ 4 parts Rue
✤ 6 oz. Rosemary
✤ 3 oz. Vetivert
✤ 2 tbsp. Hyssop
✤ Sprig of Mistletoe

INSTRUCTIONS:

In a cauldron or large pot, add 4 parts Rue, 6 oz. Rosemary, 3 oz. Vetivert, 2 tbsp. Hyssop, and the sprig of Mistletoe.

Fill the pot with enough water to cover the herbs.

Bring the mixture to a boil, then reduce the heat and let it simmer for 20-30 minutes.

Once the mixture has simmered, strain the liquid into a bowl or jar, discarding the herbs.

Anointing the House

Using a small brush or your fingers, anoint each window and door of your house with the brew. As you do so, chant:

"Herbs of power, brewed so fine,
Guard this home, with strength divine.
Evil flee from every door,
Let harm enter here no more."

Sprinkling the Corners

Sprinkle the remaining brew at the four corners of your house, forming a protective barrier. As you sprinkle, chant:

"North, South, East, and West,
Keep this home safe and blessed.
By this brew, protection's spun,
Guard this place 'til task is done."

NOTES

Protection for a Love Interest

The purpose of this spell is to shield a romantic interest from danger and bad influences. You can ensure your beloved's safety and well-being by calling forth the Goddess' protecting energy and erecting a barrier around them.

REQUIREMENTS:

✼ A picture of your love interest (optional)

INSTRUCTIONS:

Find a quiet and undisturbed place where you can perform this spell without interruptions. Arrange a picture of your love interest (if available) on a small table or altar.

Meditate briefly to center yourself. Focus on a clear image of your love interest in your mind. Visualize the Goddess standing protectively over them, forming a shield of light.

Concentrate and chant the following incantation, allowing your energy to build. Feel the power of your words and intent taking form:

"Blessed Goddess, up above,
Shield my heart's desire, my true love.
Watch over him as you do for me,
Protect him with your energy."

As you chant, visualize a protective shield forming around your love interest, glowing with the Goddess's divine light.

Continue chanting with heartfelt intent:

"Blessed Goddess, if he doesn't know,
My love for him, please let it show.
Thank you, Mother, for your grace,
Protect him in your loving embrace."

Complete the chant with a final invocation:

"You know how much he means to me,
Keep him safe and trouble-free."

Take a moment to sense the protective energy surrounding your love interest. Trust that the Goddess is watching over them.

NOTES

Protection in the Snow

This spell is intended to keep you secure, stable, and warm during the winter months. You can make a potent charm that you can carry with you by imbuing each ingredient with magical purpose.

REQUIREMENTS:

❀ One peppercorn
❀ A pinch of salt
❀ A pinch of powdered ginger
❀ A pinch of powdered cloves
❀ A small square of red cotton cloth

INSTRUCTIONS:

Find a quiet and undisturbed place to perform the spell. Arrange your tools and ingredients on a small table or altar.

Place the peppercorn in a bowl, saying:

"Peppercorn, I charge thee,
With protection, guard and shield me."

Add the pinch of salt to the bowl, saying:

"Salt of earth, I charge thee,
With stability, ground and steady me."

Add the pinch of powdered ginger, saying:

"Ginger warm, I charge thee,
With warmth and comfort, surround me."

Add the pinch of powdered cloves, saying:

"Cloves of spice, I charge thee,
With protection, keep harm from me."

With your fingers, mix the assembled spices and salt, visualizing a protective aura surrounding you. Focus on having a safe and guarded winter season.

Transfer the mixed herbs to the center of the red cloth square. Fold the cloth in half, then in half again, and sew up the ends securely.

Keep this charm with you during the snowy season to benefit from its protective energies.

Make a new charm each winter to ensure continued protection.

NOTES

Protection Oil No 1

REQUIREMENTS:

❁ Base oil (sweet almond oil, jojoba, sesame, etc.)
❁ Three of the following herbs or essential oils: rue, rosemary, angelica, bay, basil, fennel, sage, mugwort, vervain
❁ A glass bottle

INSTRUCTIONS:

Find a quiet and undisturbed place where you can prepare this oil without interruptions. Arrange your ingredients and tools on a small table or altar.

Choose any three of the following herbs or essential oils: rue, rosemary, angelica, bay, basil, fennel, sage, mugwort, or vervain.

Pour the base oil into a glass bottle. Add the selected herbs or essential oils into the bottle, ensuring they are fully submerged in the oil.

Hold the bottle in your hands and visualize a protective light surrounding it. Chant with intent:

"Herbs of power, oil so pure,
Blend together, protection sure.
Infuse this oil with strength and might,
Guard me well, both day and night."

Allow the herbs to mix and steep in the oil for one week. Handle the bottle frequently, projecting protective energy into the mixture.

Using the Oil

Use the oil to anoint your body, doorways, windows, or any object you wish to protect. As you do, visualize a protective barrier forming around you or the object.

While anointing, chant with intent:

"Oil of protection, strong and true,
Guard me now in all I do.
By your power, I am shielded,
Harm to none, this spell is wielded."

NOTES

Protection Oil No 2

REQUIREMENTS:

❋ 1 dram Patchouli Oil
❋ 1 dram Frankincense Oil
❋ 1 dram Myrrh Oil
❋ 1 teaspoon broken pieces of Mandrake Root
❋ 3 heaping teaspoons coarse Sea Salt
❋ An enamel pan
❋ Small bottles for storage

INSTRUCTIONS:

Find a quiet and undisturbed place where you can prepare the protection oil without interruptions. Arrange your tools and ingredients on a small table or altar.

Cleanse and consecrate your space and tools. Light a candle or incense to create a sacred atmosphere.

In the enamel pan, combine 1 dram of Patchouli Oil, 1 dram of Frankincense Oil, and 1 dram of Myrrh Oil. As you add each oil. Chant:

"Patchouli deep, Frankincense bright,
Myrrh of wisdom, guard with might."

Add 1 teaspoon of broken pieces of Mandrake Root to the pan. Chant:

"Mandrake strong, with roots that bind,
Protect this space, both heart and mind."

Add 3 heaping teaspoons of coarse Sea Salt. Chant:

"Salt of earth, so pure and true,
Shield us now, in all we do."

Simmer the mixture over low heat, stirring gently. As it simmers, visualize the protective energies blending and growing stronger. Chant:

"By fire's warmth and cauldron's might,
Blend these gifts to guard and light."

Allow the mixture to cool. Once cooled, pour the oil into small bottles. Seal each bottle tightly.

Place the bottles on your altar and light a candle beside them. Close your eyes, hold your hands over the bottles, and visualize them glowing with protective energy. Chant:

"Oil of protection, strong and true,
Guard us well, in all we do.
Blessed by fire, earth, and air,
Keep us safe, beyond compare."

Leave the bottles on your altar overnight to absorb the energies.

Using the Oil

Use this oil to anoint doorways, windows, candles, or yourself to invoke protection. As you anoint, chant:

"With this oil, protection flows,
Guarding us where'er we go."

Protection Oil No 3

REQUIREMENTS:

- ❂ 1 dram-sized bottle
- ❂ 1/2 dram Sweet Almond Oil
- ❂ 3 drops Amber Oil
- ❂ 1 drop Jasmine Oil
- ❂ 7 drops Dark Musk Oil (Plain Musk may be substituted)
- ❂ 5 drops Rue Oil
- ❂ 3 small pieces Dragon's Blood Resin
- ❂ 1 pinch coarse Sea Salt

INSTRUCTIONS:

Find a quiet and undisturbed place where you can craft the protection oil without interruptions. Arrange your tools and ingredients on a small table or altar.

Before you begin, cleanse and consecrate your space and tools. Light a candle or incense to create a sacred atmosphere.

Begin by pouring 1/2 dram of Sweet Almond Oil into the dram-sized bottle. As you add the oil, visualize it as the base of your protective shield.

Add 3 drops of Amber Oil, shaking the bottle gently to mix. Chant:

> "Amber's warmth, protect and hold,
> Shield me with your light of gold."

Add 1 drop of Jasmine Oil and shake again. Chant:

> "Jasmine pure, with scent so sweet,
> Guard me from all harm I meet."

Add **7** drops of Dark Musk Oil (or Plain Musk if substituting) and shake well. Chant:

> "Musk of darkness, strong and deep,
> Protect me as I wake and sleep."

Add **5** drops of Rue Oil and shake once more. Chant:

> "Rue's defense, so strong and sure,
> Keep me safe, my spirit pure."

Drop **3** small pieces of Dragon's Blood Resin into the bottle and shake. Chant:

> "Dragon's blood, with strength so rare,
> Guard me now, beyond compare."

Finally, add a pinch of coarse Sea Salt and shake to mix. Chant:

> "Sea salt coarse, from ocean's depth,
> Protect and guard with every step."

Once all ingredients are added and mixed, seal the bottle tightly. Hold it in your hands, closing your eyes, and visualize a protective aura surrounding the bottle and its contents.

Place the bottle in a safe place on your altar and allow it to sit overnight to absorb the energies. You may also choose to bless it under the Dark Moon.

Using the Oil

Use this oil to anoint candles, doorways, windows, or yourself to invoke protection. As you anoint, chant:

> "With this oil, protection flows,
> Guarding me where'er I go."

Protection Poppet

REQUIREMENTS:

❂ Dogwood twigs and shavings

❂ Black thread

❂ Acorn

❂ Black cotton thread & stuffing

❂ Eucalyptus

❂ Sage

❂ Thyme

❂ Oak leaves

❂ Parsley

❂ Fern

❂ Birch bark

❂ Nail clippings

❂ Hair

❂ Blood (optional)

❂ Cedarwood or another protective oil

❂ Dragon's Blood ink

❂ White muslin pouch

❂ Black and white agate

❂ Rose petals

❂ Rosemary sprig

INSTRUCTIONS:

On the Full Moon, create the poppet's skeleton using dogwood twigs, binding them with black thread, and using an acorn for the head.

Three nights before the Full Moon, consecrate and grind the following herbs: eucalyptus, sage, thyme, oak leaves, parsley, dogwood shavings, fern, and birch bark. Meditate on their protective purpose. Mix in nail clippings, hair, and optionally, a few drops of blood.

On a piece of birch bark, draw the rune of "Algiz" with Dragon's Blood ink. Roll it up and tie it to the poppet's torso with black thread. Fashion clothes from your own clothing and attach some of your hair to the poppet.

On the night of the Full Moon, cast your circle and sew the clothes onto the poppet, filling it with the herbal mixture. Anoint the poppet with cedarwood or another protective oil. Place the poppet on the pentacle on your altar.

Meditate on the purpose of the poppet, then dedicate it to the South. Recite the incantation:

"Magic doll, my faithful guide,
Banish harm, let none abide.
Protect me through both day and night,
Blessed by this sacred rite.
Herbs within, empowered and strong,
Keep me safe, all the days long.
Protect me now, oh little one,
Shield from harm, let there be none.
Blessed by powers of three,
This is my will, so shall it be."

Pass the poppet through the flame to the South, the water to the West, the salt to the North, and the smoke of sandalwood to the East.

Place the poppet in a white muslin pouch with a black and white agate, some rose petals, and a rosemary sprig. Draw the rune of "Algiz" on the pouch with Dragon's Blood ink. Carry this pouch with you, recharging or changing the herbs as needed.

Protection Potion (Wash)

REQUIREMENTS:

❀ 2-4 cups of Spring Water
❀ 1 tablespoon Powdered Iron or Iron Shavings
❀ 1 teaspoon Vervain
❀ 2 tablespoons Sea Salt
❀ 2 tablespoons Frankincense
❀ 2 tablespoons Myrrh
❀ A pinch of Wolf's Hair (from a live, shedding wolf; ask a zookeeper)

INSTRUCTIONS:

Find a quiet and undisturbed place where you can prepare the potion without interruptions. Arrange your tools and ingredients on a small table or altar.

Cleanse and consecrate your space and tools. Light a candle or incense to create a sacred atmosphere.

Pour 2-4 cups of Spring Water into a cauldron or pot. As you do, chant:

*"Water pure, from earth's embrace,
Form the base of our sacred space."*

Add 1 tablespoon of Powdered Iron or Iron Shavings to the water. Stir gently, chanting:

*"Iron strong, shield and defend,
Your protection now extend."*

Add 1 teaspoon of Vervain to the mixture. Stir and chant:

"Vervain sacred, herb of might,
Guard us with your ancient light."

Add 2 tablespoons of Sea Salt, stirring as you chant:

"Salt of sea, so pure and true,
Protect and cleanse in all we do."

Add 2 tablespoons each of Frankincense and Myrrh. Stir and chant:

"Frankincense and Myrrh, wise and old,
Bless this potion, strong and bold."

Finally, add a pinch of Wolf's Hair. Stir and chant:

"Wolf's hair, spirit wild and free,
Lend your strength, protectively."

Place the cauldron or pot over low heat and allow the potion to simmer. As it simmers, visualize the ingredients blending into a powerful protective force. Chant:

"By fire's warmth, this potion blend,
Protection strong, our will extend."

Once the potion has simmered and the ingredients have melded, remove it from the heat and allow it to cool. Pour the potion into bottles and seal them tightly.

Place the bottles on your altar and light a candle beside them. Close your eyes, hold your hands over the bottles, and visualize them glowing with protective energy. Chant:

"Potion strong, protection pure,
Guard us well, now and evermore.

"Blessed by earth, water, fire, and air,
Keep us safe, beyond compare."

Leave the bottles on your altar overnight to absorb the energies.

Using the Potion

Use this potion to anoint doorways, windows, or yourself to invoke protection. As you anoint, chant:

"With this potion, protection flows,
Guarding us where'er it goes."

NOTES

Protection Spell for Loved Ones

REQUIREMENTS:

✤ One white candle
✤ Protection incense
✤ Photo(s) of your loved ones

INSTRUCTIONS:

Find a quiet and undisturbed place where you can perform this ritual without interruptions. Arrange your tools and ingredients on a small table or altar.

Light the protection incense, allowing its soothing scent to cleanse the space and prepare it for the spell.

Place the white candle on top of the photo(s) of your loved ones. As you do this, focus on your intention to protect them.

Light the white candle, symbolizing the protective light of the Goddess.

Close your eyes and visualize a radiant white light surrounding your loved ones. See this light forming a strong and impenetrable barrier, keeping them safe and secure.

With your visualization clear, chant the following incantation with heartfelt intent:

"O Goddess, protect those I love each day,
In their slumber and their play.
Bring to them smiles of pure delight,
Keep them secure in Your gentle light.
Guard them from danger and all they dread,
For they are the ones I treasure and care for.
I thank You, Goddess, for being so kind,
Your strength and power always on my mind."

Let the candle and incense burn down completely, allowing their energies to solidify the protective barrier.

Trust that the Goddess's light will continue to protect your loved ones, bringing them safety and joy.

NOTES

Protective Chant for Outdoor Spells

This is a protection incantation to keep you safe when you're out casting spells at night. To ensure your spellcasting is safe and undisturbed, you can trap any evil around you by drawing a glowing pentagram in the air and calling upon the moon's protection.

Requirements:

- A blessed (preferably pointy) object (such as a wand)

Instructions:

Find a quiet and undisturbed outdoor place where you can perform this spell without interruptions. Hold your blessed object, such as a wand, ready in your hand.

Using your blessed object, draw a pentagram in the air. As you do, visualize the pentagram glowing brightly, trapping any evil within its bounds.

With clear intent and focus, chant:

"Hail, fair moon, ruler of night,
Guard me and mine till morning's light."

Take a moment to sense the protective energy surrounding you. Trust that the glowing pentagram and the moon's power are safeguarding you.

Confident in your protection, proceed with the outdoor spells you wish to perform.

Protective Ward for a Ring

This incantation is intended to establish an invisible defence for a ring, endowing it with the capability to shield against injury. By evoking the elements and the illumination of the full moon, you affix a protective charm to the ring.

REQUIREMENTS:

❀ A ring to be enchanted
❀ Stones and symbols of earth
❀ A shell or crystal dish
❀ Water
❀ Salt

INSTRUCTIONS:

Find a quiet and undisturbed place to perform the spell. Arrange your tools and ingredients on a small table or altar.

Place the ring in the North of the room, symbolizing the element of earth. Surround it with stones and symbols representing earth.

In a shell or crystal dish filled with water, mix in some salt. Hold the ring over the dish and chant:

> "Creature of earth, hear my plea,
> Protect from harm, I ask of thee.
> Into this water, the ring I lay,
> Bind protection, keep evil at bay."

Leave the ring in the salt water overnight, ensuring it is bathed in the light of the full moon. This will charge the ring with protective energy.

In the morning, wash the salt water off the ring. Clear away the stones and symbols, then wear the ring to benefit from its protective ward.

104

Removing the Ward

To remove the spell, place the ring in the South of the room, symbolizing release.

Say the following words to lift the spell:

"With gratitude for protection shown,
I release this spell, now be it known."

Leave the ring overnight in a window during the new moon to complete the spell removal.

NOTES

Quick Shield of Safety

This powerful protection spell creates a shield of safety around you, binding protective energy on all sides. By chanting the incantation, you invoke a magical ward that guards you from harm.

INSTRUCTIONS:

Find a quiet and undisturbed place where you can perform this spell without interruptions. Stand in the center of your space and focus your intent.

With clear intent and focus, chant:

> "A spell of safety here I weave,
> A ward of might, no harm to cleave.
> A shield before me, and behind,
> To right and left, protection bind.
> No ill shall come, nor harm me near,
> By Her Rede, I hold most dear."

As you chant, visualize a glowing shield forming around you, creating a protective barrier on all sides.

Take a moment to sense the protective energy surrounding you. Trust that the shield will guard you from all harm.

NOTES

Safety Map for Travels

REQUIREMENTS:

❋ Map of your travel area
❋ Green pen
❋ White chalk
❋ Three small crystals (clear quartz, amethyst, or any protective stone)
❋ White ribbon

INSTRUCTIONS:

Cast a protective circle to ensure a sacred and safe space for your spell.

Spread out the map of the area through which you will be traveling.

Using the green pen, carefully trace the route you plan to take.

Take the white chalk and lightly color over the entire itinerary, visualizing the chalk as a glowing light of protection illuminating your path.

As you do this, recite the following chant:

> Guard and guide our journey true,
> Bless this road for me and you.
> See us safely to our goal,
> Keep us safe, complete and whole.

Place the three small crystals on the map.

Fold the map carefully, enclosing the crystals inside.

Tie the folded map with the white ribbon, securing the crystals and your protective intentions.

Keep the enchanted map on your altar or in a safe place until you return from your journey.

Shield of Fire

REQUIREMENTS:

❈ One candle at each compass point (North, South, East, West)
❈ Athame

INSTRUCTIONS:

Cast the sacred circle.

Invoke the presence of the God and Goddess.

Statement of Intent:

On this sacred night, I call upon the powers of fire to shield and protect me from all harm, be it physical, mental, emotional, or spiritual.

Begin in the South.

Light the candle, proclaiming:

> "From the South, no harm shall come to me!"

Visualize a flaming barrier forming on that side, protecting you.

Move to the West.

Light the candle, declaring:

> "From the West, no harm shall come to me!"

Envision the protective flame growing stronger.

Proceed to the North.

Light the candle, stating:

> "From the North, no harm shall come to me!"

108

See the wall of fire becoming even more powerful.

Finally, go to the East.

Light the candle, announcing:

"From the East, no harm shall come to me!"

Imagine the shield of flames surrounding you completely.

Elevate the Southern candle towards the sky, shouting:

"From above, no harm shall come to me!"

Lower it to the ground, saying:

"From below, no harm shall come to me!"

Sit in the center of your circle, gazing at the burning candles.

Focus on the flames, feeling their energy forming an impenetrable shield around you.

Meditate on this protective barrier, knowing it can be summoned whenever you feel threatened.

Partake in cakes and ale to replenish your energy (bread and wine or juice).

Release the circle, expressing gratitude to the God and Goddess for their protection and presence.

Address each direction in turn:

"Guardians of the East (South, West, North),
Powers of Air (Fire, Water, Earth),
I thank you for your presence in my circle.
I seek your blessing as you depart.
May peace prevail between us now and forever."

Raise your Athame to the sky, then touch it to the earth. Open your arms wide and proclaim:

"The circle is open, yet remains unbroken,
May the peace of the Lord and Lady dwell in my heart.
Forevermore, blessed be!"

Shielding Stone of Saturn

With the help of this spell, you can create a strong charm that will protect you from harm by charging a protective stone with Saturn's force. You can give the stone defensive energy by centring and anchoring oneself inside a circle of salt.

REQUIREMENTS:

❁ A small stone of Saturn correspondence (black tourmaline, Apache tears, or snowflake obsidian)

❁ Salt

INSTRUCTIONS:

Find a quiet outdoor place where you can perform this spell without interruptions. Arrange your ingredients and tools on a small table or altar.

Sprinkle a circle of salt on the ground, large enough for you to sit inside. This circle will serve as your sacred space for the ritual.

Choose a small stone of Saturn correspondence, such as black tourmaline, Apache tears, or snowflake obsidian. Alternatively, find any dark-colored stone from the earth that feels solid, stable, and strong.

Sit inside the circle of salt, holding your chosen stone. Close your eyes, ground, and center yourself by drawing Earth energy within you.

Visualize rings of energy swirling around the stone you hold. See these rings building and increasing in strength, surrounding and emanating from you. Chant:

> "Stone of Saturn, dark and strong,
> Shield me well, protect from wrong.
> Rings of power, swirling bright,
> Guard me through both day and night."

Within these rings of energy, sense yourself becoming strong, solid, secure, and shielded from harm. Let the energy infuse the stone with protective power.

Keep the charged stone with you as a charm of protection. It will act as a shield against negative energies and harm.

Whenever you feel the need for extra protection, hold your stone and visualize the rings of energy surrounding you once more.

NOTES

Simmering Potpourri of Protection

This enchanting simmering potpourri generates a protective aura around your residence, shielding it from harmful energies and undesirable influences. The amalgamated properties of these herbs will repel danger and promote a harmonious atmosphere.

REQUIREMENTS:

❁ 4 tablespoons rosemary
❁ 3 bay leaves
❁ 1 tablespoon basil
❁ 1 tablespoon sage
❁ 1 tablespoon fennel seeds
❁ 1 teaspoon dill seeds
❁ 1 teaspoon juniper berries
❁ A pinch of dried garlic (optional)

INSTRUCTIONS:

Collect all the listed herbs and place them in a small bowl.

Using your hands, mix the herbs together gently. As you blend them, visualize your home being enveloped by a shield of protective energy.

Focus your intentions on protection and safety. Channel your protective energies into the herbs, infusing them with your power.

Add 2 cups of water to a non-metallic pan or a simmering potpourri pot.

Slowly add the charged herbs to the simmering water. As you do, chant softly:

"Herbs of power, strong and true,
Protect this home in all we do.
Ward off harm and keep us safe,
Fill our space with your embrace."

112

Let the potpourri simmer over low heat for at least half an hour. As it simmers, envision the protective energies spreading throughout your home, creating a sanctuary of peace and safety.

If you wish to simmer the potpourri longer, add more water as needed to maintain the infusion.

NOTES

Talisman to Protect Another

REQUIREMENTS:

❀ A piece of topaz, malachite, or coral (any size or color)
❀ Small piece of pale blue or white paper
❀ Water
❀ Small box (pale blue or white)
❀ White fabric
❀ Six of the following plant parts (not the fruit): Acacia, Aloe, Angelica, Anise, Ash, Basil, Birch, Blackberry, Blueberry, Broom, Caraway, Carnation, Cedar, Cinquefoil, Clover, Cotton, Cypress, Dill, Eucalyptus, Fennel, Flax, Foxglove, Grass, Hazel, Heather, Holly, Irish Moss, Ivy, Lilac, Mandrake, Marigold, Mistletoe, Mugwort, Mulberry, Oak, Olive, Pine, Primrose, Raspberry, Rice, Rose, Rosemary, Sandalwood, Spanish Moss, Thistle, Valerian, Violet, Willow

INSTRUCTIONS:

Place the stone on the piece of paper.

Draw a circle around the stone. The more accurate the circle, the stronger the spell.

Cast a sacred circle and place the paper with the stone in the center.

Sprinkle water gently over the stone.

Visualize a white light surrounding the stone and whatever you wish to protect.

Write on the lid of the box:

"Oh benevolent Goddess, whose boundless love and strength endure, I call upon your grace to protect and secure. May [object/person to be protected] be shielded by your power divine, Kept safe from all harm, through the endless passage of time. With your unwavering care, both day and night, Guard [object/person to be protected], with your celestial light. Let them be enfolded in your embrace so pure, In your eternal protection, may they always endure."

114

Place the white fabric inside the box.

Position the stone on the fabric with the paper beneath it.

Arrange six selected plant parts around the stone.

Recite the written words on the box lid with all your heart, six times.

Close your circle.

Place the box in a secluded spot that receives sunlight for five days.

Each night at the same time (6 o'clock is recommended), take out the box and recite the words six times without opening the box.

Final Steps on the Sixth Day:

Before the time you originally performed the spell, remove the stone from the box.

Sprinkle it with water and chant the words six times.

Give the stone to the person you wish to protect, or place it near the object to be protected.

If concerned about losing the stone, hide it in the person's room.

At the same time on the sixth day, bury the plant parts and piece of paper from the box while reciting the words six times.

Thank the Goddess for her protection and blessings.

NOTES

Tarot Protection

This Tarot Protection Spell surrounds you with a protective barrier by utilising the power of particular tarot cards. You can summon heavenly guardians and create a shield of radiant light by concentrating on your requirements and calling forth the energies of these cards.

REQUIREMENTS:

❁ A tarot deck
❁ A quiet, undisturbed space

INSTRUCTIONS:

Find a quiet and undisturbed place where you can perform this ritual without interruptions. Arrange your tarot deck on a small table or altar.

Select a significator card that represents you. Place it in the center of a cross layout.

Place the Ten of Pentacles or Ten of Cups beneath the significator.

Position the Four of Wands at the base.

Place the Chariot at the top.

Position Temperance and the Star to form the arms of the cross.

Sit quietly and meditate on your protection needs. Visualize the tarot cards glowing with protective energy, forming a radiant shield around you.

With your focus clear, recite the following affirmation with intent and power:

"I call upon the power within me and around,
Sentinels of the heavens, spirits profound.
Ministering angels, come to my side,
For protection, defense, and safety I abide.
With white light, a force field is built,
Shielding me, guarding me, as I will.

116

Negative disperse, dissolve in the light,
Shadows flee, banished from sight.
Harm and danger, neutralized be,
By the touch of my glowing aura, set free.
Power within and power around,
Only peace, love, and serenity be found.
I am protected, my family too,
My home is safe, in all I do.
All travel modes, shielded in light,
So it is, so shall it be, this night!"

Envision a radiant white light emanating from the cards, enveloping you, your loved ones, and your home in a protective barrier. Feel the strength of the shield, impenetrable and glowing with divine energy.

Once you feel the protective energy solidified, thank the celestial guardians and spirits for their protection.

Leave the cards in their cross formation on your altar or return them to the deck, knowing the protection remains with you.

NOTES

The Cauldron and the Knife

This protection spell harnesses the combined powers of water and a sharp blade to shield your home from both physical and astral invasions. Perform this ceremony each evening for continual protection.

REQUIREMENTS:

❁ A cauldron, iron bucket, bowl, or pot
❁ Water
❁ A very sharp knife or Athame

INSTRUCTIONS:

Find a quiet and undisturbed place near your front door to perform this spell. Arrange your cauldron, water, and knife or Athame on a small table or altar.

Just before bed, fill the cauldron (or chosen vessel) with water.

Hold the knife or Athame above the water, focusing your intent on protection. Gently place the blade point-down into the water, chanting:

"Within this water, I place this steel,
Guard us from thief and shadows real.
No flesh nor spirit, dark or fell,
Shall enter this home where I dwell ."

Imagine a shimmering shield forming around your home, guarding it from all harm.

In the morning, carefully remove the knife, dry it, and place it in a safe location.

Without touching the water, pour it outside or down the drain. Store the cauldron away until the next evening.

NOTES

The Sand Trap Spell to Protect the Home

REQUIREMENTS:

❀ A small glass jar with a close-fitting lid (washed and dried)
❀ Two different colors of sand (e.g., grayish-white beach sand, yellowish coral sand, orangish desert sand, red volcanic sand, black obsidian sand)
❀ A spoon
❀ Two small bowls to hold the sands

PREPARATION:

Pour one type of sand into the jar until it is just over half full. Empty this sand into one bowl and label it "Sand 1."

Clean the jar and repeat the process with the second type of sand, placing it in another bowl labeled "Sand 2."

INSTRUCTIONS:

Hold your protective hand over "Sand 1." Focus on it, visualizing it humming and writhing with protective, projective energy. Touch the sand, imagining it emitting sparks of bright white light that ensnare negativity and draw it inward. Charge it with your personal power.

Repeat the process with "Sand 2."

Place the jar before you. Scoop a level spoonful of "Sand 1" and pour it into the jar while chanting:

"Trap of sand, trap the ill,
Trap the bane and evil will."

Next, scoop a level spoonful of "Sand 2" and pour it into the jar, repeating the chant:

> "Trap of sand, trap the ill,
> Trap the bane and evil will."

Continue alternating the sands, repeating the chant with each spoonful, until the jar is full.

Once the jar is filled, close the lid tightly. Hold the jar in both hands and focus your energy into it, envisioning the layers of sand creating a powerful barrier against negativity.

Hold the jar up and say with conviction:

> "By the power of earth and sand,
> This trap shall hold, my home's command.
> Negative forces be ensnared,
> Within this jar, be trapped and bared.
> With this spell, my home's defense,
> Shall keep us safe, with confidence.
> So it is spoken, so it shall be,
> Protected by this magic, blessed be."

Your sand trap spell is now complete. Place the jar near the entrance of your home or in a central location to trap and neutralize any negative energies before they can enter. May your home be guarded and protected, a sanctuary of peace and safety.

NOTES

The Witches' Bottle
(PROTECTION FROM ALL HARM)

This potent witch's bottle is crafted to safeguard you from any danger by binding it to you with your blood and sealing it with your intention. By constructing this bottle and interring it, you deflect undesirable energy from yourself and return them to their origin.

REQUIREMENTS:

❁ 1 mason jar
❁ Pins, needles, razor blades, cactus spines, rose thorns, broken glass, etc.
❁ Your blood (at least 3 drops)
❁ Your urine
❁ A small shovel or trowel for digging

INSTRUCTIONS:

Find a quiet and undisturbed place where you can perform this spell without interruptions. Arrange your tools and ingredients on a small table or altar.

Begin by placing the pins, needles, razor blades, cactus spines, rose thorns, broken glass, and other sharp objects into the mason jar. As you do, chant with intent:

> "Pins and needles, sharp and keen,
> Guard me from harm, unseen."

Prick your finger and let at least 3 drops of your blood fall into the jar, binding it to you. Chant:

> "By my blood, this charm I bind,
> Protection from harm, to me inclined."

Urinate in the jar and seal it well. As you seal the jar, focus your thoughts on protection and chant:

"Urine strong, seal this spell,
Protect me now, all harm repel."

Dig a hole in a safe and discreet location, and bury the jar. As you place it in the ground, chant:

"Lord of Life and Lady of Light,
Join me here for this rite.
This bottle made for my protection,
Bound by ancient ways and tradition.
Harm sent my way, to this grave,
Return threefold, let me be saved.
Open my ears and eyes to see,
Guard my life, protect me."

Take a moment to sense the protective energy surrounding you. Trust that the bottle will guard you from harm and redirect negative energies away from you.

NOTES

Twigs and Vine Protection Charm

This charm is designed to provide personal protection against harm and evil influences. The ritual is performed at dawn, harnessing the energy of the new day.

REQUIREMENTS:

❀ Three dried twigs of equal length
❀ Vine for binding
❀ A white candle
❀ Protection oils
❀ Incense for protection

INSTRUCTIONS:

At dawn, venture out and find three dried twigs of the same length. Ensure they are small enough to be kept as a charm. Bind them together with a vine.

At home, place the bound twigs on a table. Surround them with a white candle anointed with protection oils and light it. Light the incense of your choice for protection.

As the incense begins to produce smoke, pick up the bound twigs. Pass them through the rising smoke several times while chanting:

> "Smoke of incense, rise and twine,
> Bless these twigs with power divine.
> Protect me from harm, be my charm,
> Hold me, shield me, keep me from alarm."

Visualize a shield of protective energy enveloping the twigs, transferring your intent and will into the charm.

124

Once you feel the twigs are sufficiently charged with protective energy, place them in a small bag or pouch.

Keep the bag with you at all times for personal protection. Alternatively, hang the charm at the threshold of your home to prevent evil from entering.

NOTES

Wand Casting of Protection

This powerful incantation is intended to invoke the safeguarding force of the elements to defend against any adversary. By summoning Earth, Fire, and Water, you harness their power to construct a formidable shield.

REQUIREMENTS:

❀ Your wand
❀ A quiet, undisturbed space

INSTRUCTIONS:

Find a quiet and undisturbed place where you can perform this spell without interruptions. Stand in the center of your space with your wand.

Point your wand to the sky and chant:

> "Terra, Ignis, Aqua, hear my plea,
> Elements of astral, I summon thee.
> Earth by Divinity, Divinity by Earth,
> Grant my foe the vision, to see my worth."

Lower your wand slightly and chant:

> "With elements' might, by my side,
> In this no-rules magic, I shall abide.
> When my enemy falls, strength to see,
> This spell's power will set me free."

Point your wand back to the sky and chant:

"In no way shall this spell reverse,
Nor place upon me any curse.
By Earth, Fire, and Water's decree,
I am protected, blessed be."

Take a moment to feel the protective energy surrounding you, infused with the power of the elements.

NOTES

Ward Off Criticism and Hate

This potent charm is intended to shield a person from the hatred and judgement of others. You can build a barrier that deflects negative energy by burning an object associated with the source.

REQUIREMENTS:

❀ An item connected to the person (handwriting, picture, hair, etc.)
❀ A fireproof container
❀ Matches or a lighter

INSTRUCTIONS:

Find a quiet and undisturbed place where you can perform the spell without interruptions. Arrange your tools and ingredients on a small table or altar.

Place the item connected to the person (handwriting, picture, hair, etc.) into the fireproof container.

Light the item on fire using matches or a lighter. As it burns, focus on releasing the negative energy and shielding yourself from harm.

As the item burns, chant the following words with intent and power:

"Away from me, your words and hate,
Your criticism I dissipate.
Burn away, let flames consume,
Protect me now, let love resume."

See the flames transforming the negative energy into a protective shield that surrounds you, deflecting any further harm.

Once the item is fully burned, take a moment to feel the protective energy around you. Trust that you are now shielded from criticism and hate.

Safely dispose of the ashes away from your home, symbolizing the removal of negativity from your life.

NOTES

Wreath of Protection

This enchanted protective wreath functions as a formidable barrier against adverse energy and harmful entities. Composed of powerful herbs and flowers, it not only protects your home but also enhances the aesthetic appeal of your environment.

REQUIREMENTS:

❀ Several long branches of fresh rosemary (1-2 feet long)
❀ Fine green cotton thread
❀ Extra sprigs of rosemary
❀ Dried seed heads of rue, dill, and fennel
❀ Fresh protective flowers (snapdragons, cyclamen, garlic flowers, marigolds, carnations, or roses)
❀ Red ribbon
❀ String or fine steel wire for hanging

INSTRUCTIONS:

Take the fresh rosemary branches and shape them into a circle. Secure the branches together using the fine green cotton thread.

Use extra sprigs of rosemary to fill out the wreath, tying them securely to the main body with the thread.

Insert the dried seed heads of rue, dill, and fennel into the wreath for additional protection.

Ensure the herbs are evenly distributed and firmly attached, creating a well-balanced and full appearance.

Choose 3, 7, or 9 protective flowers and carefully poke them into the wreath.

Use flowers such as snapdragons, cyclamen, garlic flowers, marigolds, carnations, or roses for added protection and beauty.

Tie a red ribbon into a bow at the top or bottom of the wreath for an extra protective touch.

Attach a string or fine steel wire to the wreath to hang it securely.

Hold the wreath in your hands and close your eyes.

Visualize a protective light infusing the wreath, making it glow with powerful, protective energy.

Recite the following chant to empower the wreath:

> "Rosemary, dill, fennel so bright,
> Guard this home both day and night.
> Herbs and flowers, pure and strong,
> Protect us here where you belong."

Place the wreath over the hearth, on the door, or in a window—anywhere protection is needed.

As you hang it, envision a barrier forming around your home, keeping all negativity and harm at bay.

NOTES

BOOKS BY THIS AUTHOR

- The Protection Bible - The Essential Book of Protection Spells and Magic
- The Essential Book of Binding Spells and Magic
- The Essential Book of Cleansing, Blessing, and Purification Spells and Magic
- The Essential Book of Healing Spells and Magic
- The Essential Book of Household Spells and Magic
- The Essential Book of Love Spells and Magic

MORE BOOKS BY EREBUS SOCIETY

The Standard Book of Candle Magic
by K.P. Theodore

In The Standard Book of Candle Magic you will learn about the use of candles in magical traditions, the meanings of colours so you can create your own candle magic rituals, how to prepare for magical practice, how to cast a standard circle, and over 30 Candle Magic spells for your everyday magical needs.

The Standard Book of Meditation
by K.P. Theodore

Within the pages of this book, you will find a diverse array of meditation techniques waiting to be explored. From breath awareness to body scan, loving-kindness to visualization, the author has meticulously assembled a rich tapestry of practices that invite you to embark on a transformative inner journey.

Wandlore -
A Guide for the Apprentice Wandmaker
by K.P. Theodore

Delve into the ancient and intricate art of wandmaking with this comprehensive guide to the origins, properties, and crafting of magick wands. This book serves as both an introduction to wandlore and a hands-on manual for those who aspire to become skilled wand makers.

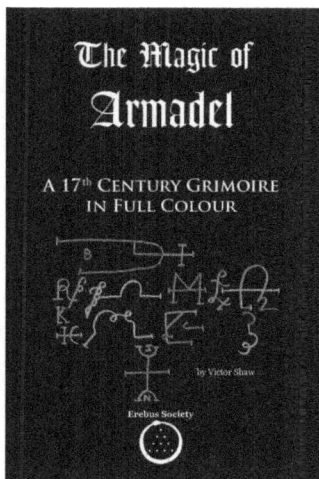

The Magic of Armadel – A 17th Century Grimoire in Full Colour
by Victor Shaw

The Grimoire of Armadel is a book of Celestial Magick and contains information, seals, and sigils of Angels, Demons and other Celestial Spirits.

It is classed as a Christian/Theistic Grimoire, and it was first translated by S.L. McGregor Mathers in the late 1890's from the original French and Latin manuscript that can be found in the Bibliotheque l'Arsenal in Paris.

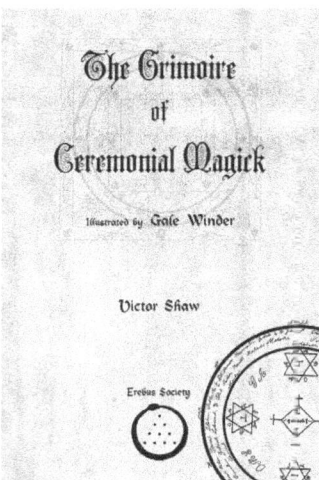

The Grimoire of Ceremonial Magick
by Victor Shaw

This book is a collection of passages, rites, practices, and rituals from various famous Grimoires. It is a cluster of the most obscure and powerful invocations, ceremonies, and pacts, and it explains their history and origins while it refutes certain myths surrounding Ancient Grimoires, and discusses the theology therein.

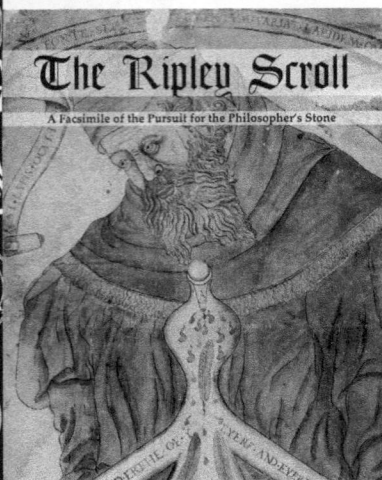

The Ripley Scroll: A Facsimile of the Pursuit for the Philosopher's Stone
by Victor Shaw

The 'Ripley scroll' or 'Ripley Scrowle' is a paramount alchemical work of the 15th century as it depicts the mystical and laborious process for the pursuit of the Philosopher's Stone. A legendary substance that can turn base metals into gold and can also be used in the making of the elixir of life, providing its possessor with prolonged life or even Immortality.

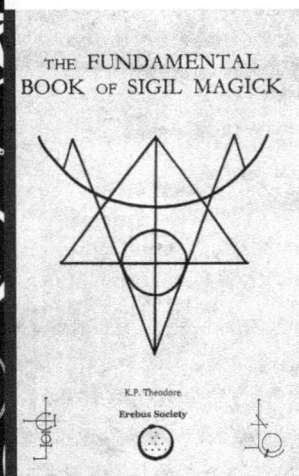

The Fundamental Book of Sigil Magick
by K.P. Theodore

This book serves as a textbook for those who wish to study the art of Sigil Magick. In its pages you will find information about the different kinds of sigils, their use, activation techniques and how to create custom tailored sigils from scratch.

Learn how to captivate emotions, empower the mind, create mental barriers, re-program the brain and alter consciousness by the use of "Mental Sigils".

The Accelerated Necromancer
by Gavin Fox

Necromancy has long been misunderstood, reduced to taboo and superstition. In this insightful work, Gavin redefines the practice, blending witchcraft and chaos magick to offer a responsible, spiritually enriching path.

With practical techniques, seasonal rites, and a fresh take on working with the dead, this book is a must-read for those seeking to walk the shadows with wisdom and reverence.